FRAGMENTS OF HELL
Israeli Holocaust Literature

FRAGMENTS OF HELL
Israeli Holocaust Literature

───────── ─────────

DVIR ABRAMOVICH

This book was published with the generous assistance of the Ziva Shavitsky Foundation for Jewish Studies.

Library of Congress Cataloging-in-Publication Data

Names: Abramovich, Dvir, author.
Title: Fragments of hell : Israeli Holocaust literature / Dvir Abramovich.
Description: Boston : Academic Studies Press, 2019.
Identifiers: LCCN 2018057560 (print) | LCCN 2019000438 (ebook) | ISBN 9781644690055 (ebook) | ISBN 9781644690048 (hardcover)
Subjects: LCSH: Holocaust, Jewish (1939-1945), in literature. | Israeli literature–History and criticism.
Classification: LCC PJ5012.H65 (ebook) | LCC PJ5012.H65 A26 2019 (print) | DDC 892.409/358405318–dc23
LC record available at https://lccn.loc.gov/2018057560

ISBN 9781644692622
ISBN 9781644690055 (ebook)

Book design by Lapiz Digital Services.
On the cover: Museum Auschwitz - Holocaust Memorial Museum. By Szymon Kaczmarczyk / Shutterstock.com

Published by Academic Studies Press
28 Montfern Avenue
Brighton, MA 02135, USA
press@academicstudiespress.com
www.academicstudiespress.com

*To my beloved family, my wife Miri and children Lori and
Ethan without whom
this book would not have been completed*

Contents

INTRODUCTION ix

CHAPTER 1
Foreboding and Wishful Thinking in a Town with a Difference 1

CHAPTER 2
Our Mother Eve on a Death Train 31

CHAPTER 3
The Prophet of Wrath and Lamentation 42

CHAPTER 4
The Shoah as an Asylum 54

CHAPTER 5
And he Survived "Planet Auschwitz" 75

CHAPTER 6
A Funny and Sensitive Story about Holocaust Memory in Israel 97

BIBLIOGRAPHY 112

INDEX 121

Introduction

The literary evocations of the Nazi extermination of European Jewry and its aftermath, as well as the works that commemorate and represent that unprecedented catastrophe, are commonly and collectively referred to as Holocaust fiction. Necessarily, the portrayals involve an array of artistic expressions that, in turn, proffer different understandings, meanings, and aesthetic conceptualizations that are evaluated and judged in this study of a small number of texts. Indeed, as this book and its series of critical essays show, this is a vast and varied corpus that takes multivalent configurations and formulations—including novels, short stories, and poetry—penned by those who witnessed the incomprehensible hell-on-earth first hand, as well as the generation after, artists removed from the tragedy both geographically and chronologically, who feel compelled to relate to and to write about this calamity.

In attempting to demarcate and frame the thematic parameters for this canon, we find much merit in Leon Yudkin's expansive casting of the net:

> Holocaust literature… is writing that takes its subject and starting point from the war conducted against the Jews from 1933 to 1945. Although that is the point of origin, the continuation is less certain, less defined and less crystalized. The effects go on, and writing allows these to move in different directions. The writer as narrator may be the prime focus of the narrative or a reporter of a distant event. Such an account may be a chronicle in which the chronicler is the principal actor or a subsidiary actor. Or he may not be involved in the story at all.[1]

---

1 Leon Y. Yudkin, "Narrative Perspectives in Holocaust Literature," in *Hebrew Literature in the Wake of the Holocaust*, ed. Leon Y. Yudkin (Rutherford, NJ: Fairleigh Dickinson University Press, 1993), 13.

Another useful working definition of Shoah literature is advanced by David Roskies, who argues that it is comprised of "…all forms of writing, both documentary and discursive, and in any language, that have shaped the public memory of the Holocaust and been shaped by it."[2]

Still, today, the symbology of Auschwitz remains ever present and occupies a principal place within our cultural, artistic, political, historical, social, anthropological, theological, psychological, and philosophical discourse. The growth of a significant body of novels, stories, poems, films, and plays in the last few decades clearly demonstrates that the Shoah still encases within its midst an undeniable moral and emotional weight, and continues to yield an extraordinarily rich harvest.

Yet, dilemmas of aesthetics constantly flicker through, since Holocaust fiction is a problematic genre. Authors—familiar with George Steiner's theory that since language is inadequate to tackle the enormity of the catastrophe, silence is the appropriate response—are also mindful of the demand for truth in turning and assimilating the inexpressible destruction and monstrosity into art. Likewise, they are aware that any blurring of the borders of testimony, memory, and fiction will be perceived as sacrilege and as an immoral distortion by the survivors. One of our concerns is to explore the challenges and difficulties those who can only rely on the imagination face in fictively writing about this historical reality.

Indeed, since the end of World War II, one of the most burning questions facing authors that has remained pertinent in the debate about representation and interpretation is how does one, in the shadow of the Holocaust, come to terms and write about a tragedy that defies the imaginative capacity of the mind without falsification and exploitation? The criterion for this vexed debate—namely, the sheer impossibility of the task—was framed early on when philosopher Theodor Adorno wrote his ideologically motivated essay "Cultural Criticism and Society," in which the oft-quoted dictum "To write poetry after Auschwitz is barbaric" appears.[3] Still, the expansion of this genre is a powerful testament that silence has not been embraced as a response and that for those who choose to depict the victims' fate and the aftermath, art is not barbaric, as Adorno's single line may have suggested.

Drawing on a vast body of scholarship, this book examines, in many ways anew, how those who lived through the Holocaust or whose families perished—as well as the non-witnesses, who observed or learned about the genocide from a distance—grapple with the knotty subject of the Shoah.

---

2   David G. Roskies and Naomi Diamant, *Holocaust Literature: A History and Guide* (Waltham, MA: Brandeis University Press, 2012), 2.

3   T. W. Adorno, *Negative Dialectics*, trans. E. B. Ashton (London: Continuum, 1981), 326.

In surveying some celebrated titles—alongside more obscure, though no less compelling works—we explore the evolving characteristics of Shoah fiction, its themes, and approaches. The mosaic of writers discussed in this book confront Hitler's genocidal war against the Jews, the suffering and trauma it inflicted, and its after-effects from their own unique point of view.

No doubt, the essential strands that bind the authors spotlighted in this study are that each has inscribed the historical events into the literary record, shading in their own meanings, discourse and methods, and memorializing the victims for those who cannot or are unable to imagine them. A few had actual and direct experiences of the Holocaust; those who were not eyewitnesses or victims felt compelled to enact and transcribe the chaos, personal anguish, and tragedy that engulfed their lives because of this catastrophe. The golden thread that runs through this book is that in plunging into these important themes, in seeking to make sense of this ghastly chapter in human history and the deep wounds inflicted on the survivors and the community, the writers help the reader better understand the Holocaust by sharply rendering the landscapes of pain and trauma through their unique lenses.

In reconstructing the past and the present, the writers explore the themes of evil, dehumanization, and destruction through multiple linguistic and poetic systems. Tellingly, they recognize that language cannot easily describe the cruelties and thus offers no easy answers to the grand and difficult questions posed by the nightmarish depths of the Shoah. Evoking the suffering becomes, in the words of David Weiss Halivni, "…an act of defiance, showing that the criminals failed, that the victim still exists, and this existence is acknowledged and recognised."[4]

Here, a note of caution is warranted. It goes without saying that this book does not in any way claim to be a comprehensive or authoritative study of the cannon. Indeed, any such attempt is doomed to fail. It is our hope, at the least, that this text and its literary selections sparks a conversation and prods the reader to explore the larger canvas of works by these authors. The one common denominator that unites the authors examined in the following chapters is that while some share nationalities and recurring themes in traversing this elusive terrain, they wrote the majority of their masterpieces in Hebrew.

We argue that despite the ever-growing critical and testimonial spotlight cast on the Shoah—along with the growing wave of historical treatises and tomes—a delicate and deeply searching work that attempts to come to

---

4 David Weiss Halivni, "Holocaust Questions," *Judaism: A Quarterly Journal of Jewish Life and Thought* 46, no. 4 (Fall 1997): 476.

full reckoning with the Holocaust can afford a band of golden rays and a pathway for those desensitized by the immensity of the voluminous historical research amassed. Certainly, Holocaust literature, with its multiplicity and polyphonic array of intentions, visions, nuances, and concerns, can grant an open space for independent and meaningful reflection about the nightmare in a way that history books cannot. As one theorist shrewdly observed, "Historians are becoming more and more aware of this and recognise that writers of fiction have an important role to play here, giving voice to the partial and uncertain."[5] Equally, fiction, operating according to its tempo and rules, its own logic, and unencumbered by doctrinal boundaries can penetrate surface attitudes and probe our innermost truths, sometimes concealed by the historicity of the past, as Geoffrey Hartmann maintains: "We have learned that stories cannot be abbreviated by an intellectual method, or foreclosed by spiritual hindsight."[6]

Significantly, it is the fruits of the imaginative writer that have become the dominant form in current Holocaust discourse. In other words, it is the "novelist's crucible," to borrow from one critic, that is shaping contemporary Shoah images rather than the "historian's anvil."[7] One of the drivers for this work is the notion that, "Historians are becoming more and more aware of this and recognise that writers have a key role to play here, giving voice to the partial and uncertain."[8] More than that, Holocaust literature, seeking to depict superhuman evil, rather than nullifying or invalidating historical verity, enhances its power.[9]

This inevitably raises two questions: (1) how does one write about the catastrophe in the wake of the assault and mutilation of language and (2) how do those who mercifully were spared the Nazi genocide imaginatively fill in the blanks and reinscribe the trauma with empathy and affinity? Considering the intersection of art and the Holocaust, one is compelled to ponder the perils of such an endeavor. Such dilemmas plague any writer searching for the architecture of language and narrative, as though gazing at a screen of the past but unable to act.

---

5   Gabriel Josipovici, "Writing the Unwritable: A Debate on Holocaust Fiction," *Jewish Chronicle* 45, no. 2 (1998): 12.
6   Geoffrey Hartman, *The Longest Shadow: In the Aftermath of the Holocaust* (Bloomington, IN: Indiana University Press, 1996), 29.
7   Haim Yosef Yerushalmi, *Zakhor: Jewish History and Jewish Memory* (Seattle: University of Washington Press, 1998), 98.
8   Josipovici, "Writing the Unwritable," 12.
9   Hanna Yaoz, "Holocaust Hebrew Literature—Between the Concrete and the Mythological," in *Comprehending the Holocaust: Historical and Literary Research*, ed. Asher Cohen, Yoav Gelber, and Charlotte Wardi (New York: Peter Lang, 1988), 355.

Confronting a nightmare that seventy years later stubbornly refuses to disappear, Holocaust writers weave into their stories a tone of frustration compounded by the desire to know the unknowable, to actualize through their imagination what is lacking, casting a searching eye in the midst of the storm of their family and their nation. For these authors, embedding their anguish and grief becomes a psychological archaeology as they excavate slowly through the layers of events they cannot comprehend in the hope of etching the victim's agony into today's world. Looming large over the matrix of Shoah literature is the cardinal topos of mourning, of working through the wounded and inherited pain and trauma, and ultimately reaching for an affirmation of life.

Obviously enough, the very act of writing after Auschwitz tests the limits of representation. Any author who elects to write about the Holocaust will naturally consider the adequacy of the literary frameworks that may inadvertently transgress and violate the truth of the historical event. To wit, if we are to deploy Lyotard's analogy of the Holocaust as an earthquake that has shattered all instruments of measurement, we must accept that the atrocity has obliterated humanity's foundations and core beliefs and, along with it, its conventional tools of artistic figuration.[10] In his reasoned analysis of whether the Final Solution and the industrialized extermination perpetrated by the Third Reich foists confining limits on writers of fiction, Haydn White asserts that

> ...unless a historical story is presented as a literal presentation of real events, we cannot criticize it as being true or untrue to the facts of the matter. If it were presented as a figurative representation of real events, then the question of its truthfulness cannot be criticised as being either true or untrue to the facts of the matter... The kind of anomalies, enigmas and dead ends that met with discussion of the representation of the Holocaust are the result of a conception of a discourse that owes too much to realism that is inadequate to the representation of events, such as the Holocaust.[11]

In other words, White allows for the train of literary expression to travel through multiple stations on its thorny expedition. In doing so, he rejects those advocating for a monochromatic model of representation, arguing that "...the best way to represent the Holocaust and the experience of it may

---

10   Jean François Lyotard, *The Differend: Phrases in Dispute* (Manchester: Manchester University Press, 1988), 56.
11   Hayden White, "Historical Emplotment and the Problem of Truth," in *Probing the Limits of Representation: Nazism and the "Final Solution,"* ed. Saul Friedlander (Cambridge, MA: Harvard University Press, 1992), 40, 50.

well be by a kind of 'intransitive writing' which lays no claim to the kind of realism aspired to by the nineteenth-century historians and writers."[12]

Chapter 1 offers a close reading of the novella *Badenheim 1939*, by Aharon Appelfeld, Israel's most celebrated Shoah author. For more than four decades, Appelfeld won international acclaim for his subtle and enigmatic novels, which shimmer with premonitions of the unimaginable horror to come. His stories, which reveal unfathomable depths in the search for meaning and healing amid the chaos, usually tackle the years immediately before and after the destruction of European Jewry. *Badenheim 1939* is the laconic masterpiece that introduced the author to foreign-language readers. As one commentator astutely observed, "Appelfeld succeeds where other writers fear to go. Rather than pouring down as in a thunderstorm, the story splashes forth like drops of rain. His life is a patchwork of shadows, fleeting memories and character-rich parable."[13]

While readers may be startled by the strange silences of *Badenheim 1939* and the slow and orderly unfolding of the monstrosity that lures Jews into accepting and collaborating in their own extermination, they are also likely to be stunned by the victims' blindness to the cruel reality that the trains taking them for "resettlement" are, in fact, transporting them to the killing centers.

Like Appelfeld, Dan Pagis, whose magisterial poem "Written in Pencil in the Sealed Railway Car" forms the backbone of Chapter 2, was born in Bukovina and grew up in a German-speaking Jewish home. We discuss in detail one of the most famous Holocaust poem of modern times, which with its breathtaking ingenuity and poignancy not only overrides Adorno's mantra, but demands that the spectator listen to the testimony and pleas of the victims. Indeed, as one scholar noted, this is a poem "unlike any we have read."[14]

Employing biblical iconography and myth, Pagis defamiliarizes and transports the dramatis personae of the archetypal tale of the primordial family into the terrors of the "Final Solution," linking the Nazis' ultimate horrors to the first fratricide. As we illustrate, the six lines of this distinctive and yet universal opus meld the canonical and the historical, the abstract with the concrete. Moreover, through his searing deployment of allusion, Pagis conveys the unexpressed terrors and grief of loss through what is

---

12 White, "Historical Emplotment and the Problem of Truth," 52.
13 Joel Engelhardt, "Rediscovering Holocaust Buried Deep in Childhood," *Palm Beach Post*, December 19, 2004, 9.
14 Alan Shapir, *That Self-Forgetful Perfectly Useless Concentration* (Chicago: University of Chicago Press, 2016), 24.

unsaid, through a weeping character who chokes midway, unable to utter and articulate the ungraspable enormity of her situation. In the exploration that ensues, we probe—among an array of other motifs—how the poem's effective power derives from its direct call to the modern hearer to act, rousing us to resist the more easily assumable posture of the bystander, and to transform the mythic message relayed by Eve into the actual.

Fellow survivor Yehiel Dinur is currently regarded as arguably one of the Holocaust's most significant transcribers. Described as a "noble fighter, a legend in his own lifetime"[15] by Holocaust survivor and journalist Noah Kliger, he wrote about his experiences in Auschwitz in a series of semi-autobiographical novels that were initially dismissed as too lurid and perverse, consequently relegated to the genre of pulp fiction because of their unsavory violence and raw sexual descriptions. Yet, he was one of the first Hebrew writers to introduce the concentrationary universe to the Jewish settlement in Palestine and then to young Israeli readers in the early 1950s. Better known under the pseudonym Ka-Tzetnik 135633, Dinur came to international attention when he collapsed while giving his dramatic testimony at the 1961 Eichmann trial after being asked if he was the writer behind the nom-de-plume and why he had concealed his identity. The literary chronicles allowed Dinur to take the reader into the hellish environment of Auschwitz, which he meticulously recreates, and to observe, almost unmediated, the evil and murderous nature of the Nazis that was unleashed on their victims. Through his texts, heavily imbued with deep sincerity, Dinur sought to be a voice for the dead who could not speak, for the nameless victims with whom he deeply identified. In his book *Ha-Shaon asher me'al ha-Rosh* (1960; translated as *Star Eternal*, published 1967), the main protagonist vows that with "Your ashes which I embrace with my arms, I swear to be your voice… I will not stop to tell about you until my last breath."[16] Four of his novels—*Salamandra*, *House of Dolls*, *Atrocity*, and *Star-Eternal*—now rightly lauded as Holocaust classics, form the basis of our scrutiny in this chapter.

In the fourth chapter, we analyze *Streets of the River*, the epic volume of poems by Uri Zvi Greenberg. Widely considered as the single greatest literary response to the Holocaust in the Hebrew language, and still haunting readers today, the poems remain unmatched for their thundering force and rhetorical heights. Ablaze with apocalyptic wrath, the dramatic

---

15   Noah Kliger, "Ha-'Ish mi-Kochav ha-'Efer Aushvitz" [The Man from Auschwitz, the Planet of Ashes], *Yediot Ahronot*, July 23, 2001.
16   Ka-Tzetnik, *Shaon asher me'al ha-Rosh* [The Clock above the Head] (Tel Aviv: Hakibutz Hameuchad, 1989), 191.

series of lamentation pieces rage at the barbarity of the Nazi oppressors and the ancient tradition of anti-Semitism buried within Christianity while mourning the dead. Doubtless, even those critics who rejected Greenberg's political ideology "recognised him as the one great poet of his generation and as a superior thinker."[17] So monumental was the impact of this work that, soon after its publication, the Dean of Israeli critics, the late Baruch Kurzweil, declaimed that *Streets of the River Streets* "is the most commanding and authentic historical document of the life of the nation of Israel and the 20th century catastrophe that struck our people… it is without precedent…this book of poetry is a magnificent, singular event in our literature, the most faithful reflection of our reality, the perfect fusion of the image of loss and redemption."[18]

Employing elements and language from the Hebrew Bible and medieval poetry, Greenberg, who rejected the use of the term *Holocaust*, instead choosing "The destruction of the exiles," argues that the "Final Solution" was an inevitable and direct extension of the atrocities of the past. In other words, by drawing such equations, Greenberg mythologizes the evil of the Third Reich and its crematoria as a link in the scriptural chain dating back to the casting of Abraham into the oven in Ur. Accordingly, Greenberg, in coming to terms with the overall destruction of European Jewry and the loss of his family, suffuses the national tragedy with a scorching personal sense of guilt while at the same time confecting a magnificent vision of a messianic hope, redemption, and restoration of the Kingdom of Israel.

Next, we turn our attention to the darkly comical 1968 novel *Adam Resurrected* by Israeli author Yoram Kaniuk. As with Greenberg, Kaniuk is not a survivor of the Nazi genocide, though he listened to survival accounts during his work as a sailor on a ship that ferried the remnant from Europe to Israel. At first shunned by Israeli readers who, gripped by the euphoria of the 1967 Six-Day War, were indifferent to the suffering and brokenness of their traumatized brethren, this extraordinary book—with its blend of poetic realism, absurd humor, fantasy, and unsettling psychological portraits—is now rightly regarded as major work of Holocaust literature. The story concerns a former circus entertainer who is spared death by spending days on all fours as a dog, entertaining the camp commandant of

---

17   Yaacov Shavit, "Uri Zvi Greenberg: Conservative Revolutionarism and National Messianism," *The Jerusalem Quarterly* 48 (Fall 1988): 63–72.

18   Baruch Kurzweil, "Shirey Rechovot ha-Nehar" [Poems of the *Streets of the River*], in *Rechovot ha-Nehar le Uri Zvi Greenberg: Mechkarim ve-Te'udot* [*Streets of the River by Uri Zvi Greenberg: Research and Materials*], ed. Lipsker Avidav and Tamar Wolf Monzon (Ramat Gan: Bar Ilan University Press, 2007), 45, 53.

Auschwitz. He is also forced to play the violin to thousands of Jews who are marched to the gas chambers, including his daughter and wife.

After the war, paralyzed by extreme shame and guilt, and recovering from a nervous breakdown after he goes in search of his last surviving family member, the circus entertainer becomes the leader of a coterie of Holocaust survivors at a psychiatric center in Israel's Negev desert. To be sure, this is not a traditional Shoah tale and was clearly ahead of its time, departing from the conventionally reverential tone adopted by Israeli authors. Kaniuk navigates controversial waters, defiantly tackling uncomfortable, weighty themes such as the gruelling emotional turmoil faced by those Jews who cooperated in order to stay alive or the depiction of Israel not as the welcoming haven for the wounded victims that it was often perceived to be, but rather as a madhouse.

This book concludes with an examination of "Shoes," a canonical short story by Israeli author Etgar Keret, part of the new wave of Israeli authors that came of age in the 1990s. Renowned for his micro-fiction, the best-selling author often visits the theme of the Holocaust, dissecting the complex emotions of guilt and confusion that the Holocaust stirs and evokes in young Israelis. The tale, which employs a postmodern sensibility to deconstruct the theme of Holocaust memorialization and education in Israel, especially amongst Jewish teens, features a third-generation protagonist. Employing his trademark mordant humor, it furnishes readers with an irreverent and quirky, though sensitive, integration of Shoah traces within everyday scenarios and as an essential part of daily life.

Additionally, the text probes such grand issues as private acts of memorialization versus collective remembrance, generational and intergenerational memory, the ethics of fictionalizing genocide, and the various modalities of coping in the modern Jewish state. Certainly, Keret moves away from the Hebraic-Zionist political paradigm that dominated Israel in its first decades of existence to a more creative, albeit provocative to some, paradigm that is reflective of the contemporary Israeli zeitgeist and one that demythologizes older frames and dynamics of commemorating traumatic history. As we show, Keret's story argues that there is not a single or clear version in the typology of responses within the Jewish-Israeli orbit of transmission and memorialization of the atrocity, and that a more emphatic tone is warranted to engage with the third and fourth generations. In short, Keret is proposing a radical reconfiguration and a rethink in relation to the problematics of Holocaust remembrance in Israel as a civic ritual, advocating for its liberation from the ossified and crippling conventional discourses. As one commentator opined in relation to "Shoes":

> It isn't, in Keret's stories, that the Holocaust is treated with impropriety but rather that, for the school children who are some of his protagonists, it is a past violence that shares place with the violence of the present. It is as if Keret were asking: How does one "remember" what is, in fact, ongoing (war, strife, terror)? And what becomes of remembrance when it is a daily ritual?[19]

Keret represents the second generation, a group of artists far removed from the cataclysm, who observed the genocide from a distance and grew up in a state draped in the onerous garb of the Shoah. Refusing to forget the evils of the past, some are coming to terms with their family's and their own nexus to the Holocaust, some are healing, and some are trying to make sense of the vast sea of despair. Their prose is a sounding board for an eclectic range of cultural and political sensibilities, as well as emotional chronicles, that broaden and transcend the traditional themes of the genre. In varying degrees, by making a sizeable impact on the literary map, they dispel any notion that the tremor of Nazi Germany ended after the war, weaving several thematic strands together in writing about how difficult it is coming to terms with this catastrophe, while at the same time underlining significant changes and attitudes regarding this subject matter.

For the cadre of artists showcased in these pages, the Shoah is ever present, freighted with a wearying legacy that is compounded by the fact that they have assumed the responsibility of transmitting a burdensome memory to the generations to come: "The Holocaust continues to be part of the lives of the survivors and their family members not as an historical event, but as a traumatic experience… despite the passage of time its malignant influences have not abated."[20] To be sure, the writers examined in this book feel that they have a moral duty to bear witness to what took place so that readers are able to absorb its category-rupturing details into their consciousness while conceding that those details are almost inconceivable. Notwithstanding the fact that they may have to accept, as a condition of fact, that the Holocaust does reside in a sphere that we cannot understand, "it would be irresponsible to allow our psychological and intellectual hesitation to estrange us from that misery. The only alternative, a complex and

---

19 André Alexis, "Israel meets America: the Mythic and the Modern," *The Globe and Mail* (Canada), June 15, 2002, D29.
20 Iris Milner, *Kirchey 'Avar: Biografiya, Zehut ve-Zicharon be-Siporet ha-Dor ha-Sheni* [*Past Present: Biography, Identity, and Memory in Second-Generation Literature*] (Tel Aviv: 'Am Oved, 2003), 22.

difficult one, is to find a way of making the inconceivable conceivable until it invades our consciousness without protest or dismay."[21]

Certainly, a break with conventionalism affords authors the flexibility and sweep to try any stylistic experiments that they feel are needed, though it may upset those wishing to restrict the ambit of contemporary Holocaust expression. To put this matter more strongly, even Elie Wiesel, who was of the ardent view that only those who were "over there" know what the Holocaust means and that others never shall, has observed that one cannot embrace silence: "We must use language… We must evoke hope where there is none, and invent meaning where there is no meaning and formulate lessons for all of us to learn… the silence of memory would be a scandal."[22] Such a choice, Enzensberger warns, will result in a surrendering to cynicism (and by inference) to the moral chaos and the forces of evil that created Auschwitz.[23] As such, liming this thorny terrain forces the one who chooses to bear witness to be aware of the parameters that flash as spasmodic warning signs: "This record should not be distorted or banalized by grossly inadequate representations… There are limits to representations which should not be but can easily be transgressed. What the characteristics of such a transgression are, however, is far more intractable than our definitions have so far been able to encompass."[24]

---

21 L. Lawrence Langer, *Preempting the Holocaust* (New Haven, CT: Harvard University Press, 1998), 65.
22 Elie Wiesel, "Some Questions that Remain Open," in *Comprehending the Holocaust: Historical and Literary Research*, ed. Asher Cohen, Yoav Gelber, and Charlotte Wardi (New York: Peter Lang, 1988), 12, 18–19.
23 Cited in Lawrence L. Langer, *The Holocaust and the Literary Imagination* (New Haven, CT: Yale University Press, 1975), 2.
24 Saul Friedlander, "Trauma, Memory and Transference," in *Probing the Limits of Representation: Nazism and the "Final Solution,"* ed. Saul Friedlander (Cambridge, MA: Harvard University Press, 1992), 3.

Chapter 1

Foreboding and Wishful Thinking in a Town with a Difference

The author of more than forty novels, short stories, essays, and plays, Israel Prize Winner for Literature, and recipient of The Independent Foreign Fiction Prize, Aharon Appelfeld (1932–2018) was one of the world's most celebrated and respected Holocaust authors. As Avraham Balat remarks, Appelfeld was Israel's most

> sensitive writer, whose entire corpus is anchored in the forgotten, distant world that existed prior to the Holocaust… he is a writer who provides a mirror to the soul, who utilizes a style and substance so as to peer, through the prism of the individual, into childhood landscapes, into to the unknown world of Jews who lost their Jewish identity but who were struck by that reality.[1]

Appelfeld himself had characterized his lean, spartan parables as a "saga of Jewish sadness—long Jewish sadness that had different variations. And I am trying to pick up the last chapters."[2] Indeed, Appelfeld's literary quilt, based chiefly on his and his parents' life, has been defined as one continuous

---

1 Avram Balat, "Sipurei Yaldut 'Avuda" [Stories of the Lost Youth], *Hatzofe*, July 2, 1978. For excellent studies of the author, see Avidov Lipsker and Avi Sagi, eds., *'Esrim ve-'Arba Rei'ot be-Kitvey Aharon Appelfeld* (Ramat Gan: Bar Ilan University Press, 2010), published in English as Avi Sagi and Avidov Lipsker, ed., *Twenty-Four Readings in Aharon Appelfeld's Literary Work* (Ramat Gan: Bar Ilan University Press, 2011); and Yigal Schwartz, *Kinat ha-Yachid ve-Netzach ha-Shevet: Aharon Appelfeld—Tmunat 'Olam* [*From Individual Lament to Tribal Eternity: Aharon Appelfeld's Worldview*] (Jerusalem: Keter, 1996).
2 Michael March, "A Saga of Jewish Sadness: A Conversation with Aharon Appelfeld," *The New Presence* 16 (September 1997), 16-17.

attempt to chronicle the deracination of Jewish life in Europe.³ Though the Holocaust is Appelfeld's prevailing theme, his focus is to put a human face on the individual victims who were determinedly blind to the storm clouds gathering around them, who were caught in the web of anti-Semitism, and who were forced to assume the Jewish identity they worked so hard to rid themselves of. Appelfeld shrewdly avoids simple moral judgments, opting to remain outside the death camps or the ghettos, and guys his narratives in the abyss of postwar Europe or prior to the outbreak of World War II.

Not wanting to make obscene art of the Holocaust, he limns, albeit rarely, the heinous monstrosity of the perpetrators. Yet, at the same time, in the Appelfeld universe, the Holocaust is never a subject outside the human experience, since in many of his stories he portrays the emotionally scarred lives of the survivors, adjusting to their mundane life, after the sustained and prolonged episodes of deprivation and humiliation.

It is noteworthy that Appelfeld, whose books have been translated into more than 30 languages, was one of the first Israeli artists to address the epochal events of the Holocaust in fiction, undeterred by a publisher who rejected his first book, *Ashan* (*Smoke*, 1961) because of its confrontational subject matter. Throughout, he adopted as his primary concern the psychological trauma and pain inflicted on the survivors by the Nazi inferno rather than evoking and depicting the concentrationary universe. "Most books about the Holocaust are dealing with the Holocaust proper," Appelfeld explained. "What I'm doing is taking the Holocaust backwards and forwards, so my territory is larger."⁴ As Gila Ramras Rauch rightly notes, "It is the very absence of the direct depiction of the Holocaust experience and its omnipresence that conveys the sense of horror."⁵

In furnishing a similar assessment, Schmuel Schneider astutely maintains that in a considerable number of Appelfeld's tales one can discern a chronological continuum with the Ka-Tzetnik corpus. According to Schneider, Ka-Tzetnik centers on satanic manifestations by strikingly and repeatedly confronting the devil-victim, torturer-tortured, rapist, and those who are raped, all underlined by sexual perversions that are an expression of the unrestrained Nazi process. In contrast, Schneider

---

3   See the excellent essay on Appelfeld in Gershon Shaked, *Gal Chadash ba-Siporet ha-'Ivrit: Mason al Siporet Yisraelit Tzeira* [*New Wave in Hebrew Literature: An Essay on the Modern Israeli Literature*] (Tel Aviv: Sifriyat Hapoalim 1970), 149–67.

4   David Streitfeld, "Imagining the Unimaginable," *The Washington Post*, January 10, 1999, 15.

5   Gila Ramras Rauch, *Aharon Appelfeld: The Holocaust and Beyond* (Indianapolis, IN: Indiana University Press, 1994), 18, 19.

contends, Appelfeld's universe is dramatically more minor, populated by ordinary characters propelled toward heroism—which in its most primal, basic essence, is an existential struggle for survival—by the circumstances enveloping their world.[6] In that connection, one must also mention Uri Zvi Greenberg, whose Holocaust dirge, *Streets of the River* is evaluated in this book. Following *Ashan*'s publication, the young author was summoned to Greenberg's home, where he was excoriated and chided by the elder statesman for the book's focus on the private and personal, rather than the national:

> Greenberg told him that the Jews' gift from the creator was that of vision and prophecy. The individual was not the point. The collective must precede him… because the collective is what creates language, culture and the belief system. If the individual makes his contribution to the collective, he raises the level of the collective and that of himself too. A creative person who does not do this will not be included in the nation's memory.[7]

To be fair, Greenberg's disdain was not directed solely against Appelfeld, but was leveled at the prevailing tenor of Hebrew literature at the time. As Alan Mintz explains, according to Goldberg's polemical and artistic worldview, poetry "…takes responsibility over the lot of the nation… it is occupied with the Holocaust, with the struggle for national survival, and with Israel's sovereign statehood."[8]

It is of note that Avner Holtzman maintains that the sterling reviews of Appelfeld's early fiction, specifically his first book *Ashan*, spotlighted the striking difference between his artistic finesse and subtlety and other Holocaust depictions that were "…infected by vulgarity, sensationalism and pornography, and which pounded the reader only with the force of their thematics."[9] Holtzman then argues that the distinction foregrounded by the critics was between Ka-Tzetnik's and Appelfeld's stories, quoting, as further proof for his thesis, from a 1994 article in which Dan Miron, referring to both authors, remarked that the coarseness in the literary representations of the Shoah in Hebrew letters reached the level of pure pornography. For

---

6   Schmuel Schneider, *Existence and Memory: In the Writings of Aharon Appelfeld and Yosef Chaim Brenner and Other Writings* (Jerusalem: Carmel, 2010), 13.
7   Linda Grant, *The People On The Street: A Writer's View of Israel* (Hachette: London, 2006), 190.
8   Alan Mintz, ed., *Reading Hebrew Literature: Critical Discussions of Six Modern Texts* (Hanover: Brandeis University Press, 2003), 152.
9   Avner Holtzman, *Ahavot Tzion: Panim ba-Sifrut ha-'Ivrit ha-Chadasha* [Loves in Zion: Faces of the Modern Hebrew Literature] (Jerusalem: Carmel Publishing, 2006), 551.

Holtzman, the allusion to vulgarity in Ka-Tzetnik's portraitures by Miron is obvious.

Typically, Appelfeld's vast panoramas of vividly detailed meditations are leavened by an understated, symbolic style that is often Kafkaesque. His novels rarely tackle the Holocaust overtly or realistically, relying instead on parabolic, figurative, and surrealistic ingredients to describe the hopelessness, disorientation, and despair that enrobe the author's dramatis personae. Not infrequently, silences dot his canvas. Appelfeld's personal geysers of protestations continually explode with the visceral and tragic dimension, lodging the reader in the shocking frame of history and entrusting them with the onerous burden of supplying the human terrors the author never mentions.

Appelfeld, throughout his canon, explores the world of cultured, converted, and assimilated Jews whose complete immersion and desire for societal acceptance in Europe's elite, humanistic milieu did not shield them from the poisonous root of anti-Semitism that led to their demise. The author explained that the "blind" Jews that populate his canvas were certain that they were different from the Jews who were targeted by the Nazis:

> One of the most vicious ironies of World War II is the fact that most Jews didn't even know why they were being punished. Most of them saw themselves as an integral part of their society, as equal citizens. Many of them were patriotic Germans, Poles, Hungarians and so on. Most of them didn't know or didn't want to know they were Jewish. The Holocaust did not find a unified people, committed to its national or religious heritage. The Jews were undergoing a certain transformation, they were in the process of assimilation.[10]

Aharon Appelfeld was born on February 16, 1932 in the village of Zhadova near Chernovtsy, then located in Bukovina, Romania, and now in Ukraine. This was a region of Eastern Europe long steeped in Jewish history, folklore, and religious ideas, well known through the stories of great nineteenth-century Yiddish writers such as Shalom Alechem. However, his own parents, Michael Appelfeld and Bunia Sternberg, leaving behind the Hasidic orthodoxy and Yiddish of their parents, raised young Aharon as a secular, German-speaking boy. "I grew up," he recalled, "in an assimilated Jewish home where German was treasured. German was considered not

---

10   Esther Fuchs, *Encounters with Israeli Authors* (Marblehead, MA: Micha Publications, 1982), 58.

only a language but also a culture. All around us lived masses of Jews who spoke Yiddish, but in our house Yiddish was absolutely forbidden. I grew up with the feeling that anything Jewish was blemished."[11] In fact, Appelfeld revealed that he did not know that he was Jewish, that it was a secret in the home.

It was only later in life, after Appelfeld had reached Palestine and began to teach himself Hebrew, that he came to learn about his Jewish background. As such, when he writes about Judaism during those days before World War II, during the Holocaust, and its immediate aftermath in Europe, the faith is articulated in a different way than his own private inner feelings and remembered images of boyhood experiences. These are images in the sense of vague and material perceptions, earthy and domestic smells, nonverbal sounds, natural and man-made textures, and inviting and repellent tastes.

With only one year of formal schooling, Appelfeld grew up speaking not just the literary German his parents spoke at home, but the Romanian, Yiddish, and Ruthenian languages that he heard in the neighborhood and in the forests. His memories, therefore, though often multilingual, are those both of an uneducated and naïve child and of a person feeling the world viscerally, in a state of shock, a world that has disappeared and exists for him in fragments of memory and inarticulate feelings. Here is how Appelfeld put it in an interview with David B. Green, taking the kind of memory arousal described in Marcel Proust's *Remembrance of Things Past* (Appelfeld has confessed that, "I am writing from memory like Proust"[12]) even further from an intellectualized sensory perception:

> A great deal of my memory is in my body, in my senses, not my mind. What I mean is that much of what I experienced in these years is in my body—in my legs, my arms, my hair, in my ears—and that's an important source. Say I feel dampness in the rain that takes me to those same days. On cold days, I'm back in those days, back in the war.[13]

More so than other survivors of the Shoah, Appelfeld has a deep-seated distrust of language, logic, and words. Critics, following the writer's own

---

11   Daniel R. Schwartz, "Aharon Appelfeld's Parables," in *Imagining the Holocaust*, by Daniel R. Schwartz (New York: St. Martin's Press, 1999), 249.
12   Herbert Mitgang, *Words Still Count With Me: A Chronicle of Literary Conversations* (New York: W. W. Norton & Company, 1995), 237.
13   David B. Green, "Questions & Answers: A Conversation with Aharon Appelfeld," *Haaretz*, April 5, 2005, accessed August 8, 2018, https://www.haaretz.com/life/books/1.5100334.

confessions in the interviews, see his literary texts as an attempt to speak in "silence, muteness and stuttering."[14]

At the age of eight, his idyllic world collapsed as World War II closed in with its apocalyptic waves of invasion. He heard his mother Bonia's screams as she was murdered in the street when the Germans reached the city of Chernovtsy. He and his father Michael were first sent to a ghetto in his native Chernovtsy, and were later sent to a Nazi labor camp in Transnistria. When the two were separated shortly afterwards, Appelfeld fled into the forests and spent the next three years precariously living among peasants and horse thieves. In the harsh winters, he claimed to be a Romanian Christian orphan named Janek and worked for local peasants, a band of horse thieves, and witches for food and shelter.[15] For a time, too, he found refuge in the home of a prostitute, chopping wood and hiding in her closet by day, listening to her entertain clients by night.

As the war drew to a close and the Russians came to liberate the Jews in 1944, Appelfeld, now in his early teens, joined the Soviet army as kitchen boy. At war's end, he returned to his hometown to discover that it was empty. He eventually made his way to Italy with other survivors, where he lived with a monk who taught him Italian and French. He then joined up with other survivors at a transit camp and eventually sailed for Palestine, arriving there in 1947. Like other children who had been traumatized by their ordeal, Appelfeld was emotionally confused, socially alone, and intellectually ill-equipped to deal with the turmoil of Palestine, not least when fighting in the 1948 War of Independence.

Yet survive he did, and was sent to live on a kibbutz. Twenty years after being separated from his father and after long assuming him dead, Appelfeld met up with his father, who was working in an orchard at the time. Though he still claims to be unable to write about this reunion, Appelfeld does credit this episode as helping him come to grips with, regain, and reconstruct many lost memories of his family before the age of eight.

Appelfeld studied philosophy and Yiddish literature at the Hebrew University of Jerusalem and served for many years as a professor of literature at Ben Gurion University of the Negev. He recalls how the accusatory questions from the native-born Israelis thrust at members of his generation drew them into a life of deep denial and stillness:

---

14 Man Booker Prize, "Aharon Appelfeld," accessed August 18, 2016, http://themanbookerprize.com/author/aharon-appelfeld.
15 William Giraldi, "Grasping for Words, Grappling with the Past." *The New Republic*, May 13, 2014, accessed August 8, 2018, https://newrepublic.com/article/117739/aharon-appelfelds-suddenly-love-writing-and-holocaust.

So, we learned silence. It was not easy to keep silent. But it was a good way out for all of us. For what, when all is said and done, was there to tell… There was a desire to forget, to bury the bitter memories deep in the bedrock of the soul, in a place where no stranger's eyes, not even our own, could get to them… How many years did that violent repression continue? Every year it changed colours, and covered another region of life. The moment a memory or a scrap of memory was about to float upwards we would combat it as one does battle with evil spirits."[16]

Though rejecting the label of a Holocaust writer—"I write more about individuals than about the Holocaust,"[17]—Appelfeld has stated that the European catastrophe that befell the Jews can never be overtold in fiction since it has become a metaphor for the twentieth century: "There cannot be an end to speaking and writing about."[18] Describing himself as a Jewish writer, Appelfeld sets out the key themes that stud his pages as, "…the uprooted, orphans, the war."[19] Indeed, as Shaked appositely observes, Appelfeld was the first author in Hebrew literature to integrate into his canvass, "…refugees, the elderly, women, children, the uprooted, and those who were persecuted, terrified and broken."[20]

The haunting *Badenheim 1939*,[21] on which the author spent a year and a half crafting,[22] was the first of Appelfeld's work to be translated into English. Winner of the National Jewish Book Award for Fiction, it has been lauded as "the greatest novel of the Holocaust, largely because it deals with

---

16 Aharon Appelfeld, "The Awakening," in *Holocaust Remembrance: The Shapes of Memory*, ed. Geoffrey H. Hartman, 150–51 (Cambridge, Blackwell, 1994).
17 Herbert Mitgang, "Writing Holocaust Memories," *The New York Times*, November 15, 1986.
18 Appelfeld, "The Awakening," 15.
19 Mitgang, "Writing Holocaust Memories."
20 Gershon Shaked, *Modern Hebrew Literature* (New Milford, CT: Toby Press, 2008), 220.
21 First published in Hebrew in 1978 (Aharon Appelfeld, *Badenheim 'Ir Nofesh* [Tel Aviv: Hakibutz Hameuchad, 1978]). I am using the English translation to be found in Aharon Appelfeld, *Badenheim 1939* (London: J. M. Dent & Sons, 1980).
22 Ann Parson, "Interview: Aharon Appelfeld," *Boston Review* (December 1982), accessed August 8, 2018, http://bostonreview.net/archives/BR07.6/appelfeld.html. The novella was published in Appelfeld's book *Shanim ve-Sha'ot* [*Years and Hours*] (Tel Aviv: Hakibutz Hameuchad, 1975).

it indirectly, through allegory and even satire"[23] and as an "almost perfect novel."[24] There seems to have been little or no reaction to the Hebrew original of Appelfeld's novel that first appeared in print in 1978. If anything, it seemed puzzling and off-putting for the very reasons that make it an outstanding and insightful novel: its odd tone, its focal displacements, its hallucinatory language, its awkward structure, its superficial characters, and its nonlinear narrative. Only since its appearance in English has it drawn critical attention and acclaim.

A host of theorists have puzzled over what genre to place it in—allegory, parable, fable, satire, dream-vision—as it seems to defy any easy categorization. What everyone seems to agree on is that *Badenheim 1939*—with its sharply drawn, evocative vignettes—is a literary masterpiece of the twentieth century and belongs side by side with the classic books on the Holocaust, whether autobiographies or works of fiction. In various ways, *Badenheim 1939* contains the hallmarks of Appelfeld's subsequent oeuvre, most noticeably that the Holocaust, Hitler, Nazis, and concentration camps are never mentioned, only vaguely suggested in obscure and cryptic incidents: "The reader expecting a stark confrontation with the atrocities of the death camp did not find it in that book. Its absence was actually the enigmatic source of terror."[25]

Appelfeld has advanced the following explanation for the emotional anchor of the text: "Wonderful people, middle-class Jews who thought themselves European—who cheated themselves by believing that no one knew they were Jewish. They were sure that Jewishness doesn't mean anything to the surroundings. This was a self-deception, a great self-deception which I wanted to explore."[26] Indeed, what chiefly concerns Appelfeld is the life of assimilated Jews who were summarily deprived of their freedom and arbitrarily divested of the delusion that theirs was a civilized world, operating according to civilized rules. In another interview, he underlined the autobiographical thread that dapples the story:

---

23 Linda Grant, "Saturday Review: Essay: In the Zone of the Living," *The Guardian*, January 31, 2004. Can literature address the conflict in the Middle East? In this article, Linda Grant asks some of Israel's best-known writers whether fiction has a duty to reflect the unfolding catastrophe in the region.

24 David Mirsky, "The Noose Slowly Tightens," *Southern Jewish Weekly*, September 25, 1981.

25 J. Arnold Band, "Foreword," in *Aharon Appelfeld: From Individual Lament to Tribal Eternity*, by Yigal Schwartz. (Hanover, NH: Brandeis University Press, 2001), xii.

26 March, "A Saga of Jewish Sadness," 16.

> The atmosphere of unreality in my books—the self-delusion of the Jews—was actually *there* in Germany of 1939. One day you were a citizen, a part of the culture… the next day you were an enemy. I was young then, but I can still remember my father's face as he was put in a cattle truck. It was an expression of absolute… *disbelief*. And that is why I wrote "Badenheim 1939" in the way I did. You see… the disasters in Jewish history are too big. They are beyond tragedy. So, I had to find another form…

Denuded of historical detail, and made all the more chilling by the readers' knowledge of what is to come in the darkening landscape of Europe, the novel begins in an ordinary and matter-of-fact manner: "Spring returned to Badenheim."[27] As in every year, a cast of urbane, sophisticated, assimilated Jews from Vienna arrive for their regular summer holidays in the fictional Austrian resort town of Badenheim. There is Yanuka, a child prodigy, a Rabbi, an historian, twin youths who recite poetry by Rilke about death, a travelling salesman, and the divorced wife of an army general.

The time is menacingly either just before or after the *Anschluss*—the absorption of Austria into the German Reich—and, therefore, the imposition immediately of all the racial laws already in place since the Nazis took over in Germany. Many of the characters are not granted names, signifying their symbolic, all-purpose function. The reader apprehends the momentous historical events swirling around the author's heroes—*Anschluss, Nacht und Nebel* (a directive issued by Hitler on December 7, 1941 targeting political activists and resistance "helpers" in World War II to be imprisoned or killed)—and the horrors that await them.

Yet, it seems that none of the holiday makers, immersed in their daily trivia, seem to know or care about the political events that are about to change their lives forever. Instead, as they usually do during their summers in the spa, the well-to-do Jews are engrossed in academic discussion of Buber or talk about trivial events in their private lives, their health problems, rivalries, the warm weather, the walks through the nearby forests, and the expectation of a series of concerts to be put on—one of the main drawing cards to the spa—aside from the medicinal waters. They wait for the guest artists to come so that the musical entertainment may begin. There are delays and the concert series is cancelled, and they continue to wonder why.

The unrelentingly tragic and nightmarish portrait of dislocation and self-deception begins to ripen when, ominously, the mysterious and Kafkaesque Sanitation Department speedily invades the town. The faceless and bland uniformed inspectors—who are never referred to as

---

27 Appelfeld, *Badenheim 1939*, 1.

Nazis—suddenly appear and rigorously prowl the town. Endowed with special and absolute powers to investigate the businesses in town, they commence a meticulous check of the residents, regular vacationers, and townspeople, who, as it turns out, are all Jewish. Aptly named, the Sanitation Department views and treats the vacationers in Badenheim as if they are an infection that must be isolated, cleaned, and then purged.

Almost imperceptibly to the Jewish residents and visitors to Badenheim, things do begin to change. The so-called Sanitation Department, which seems manifestly an ironic name for the Nazi officials who are on the verge of making Austria *Jüdenrein* (cleansed of Jews), starts to make inspections of public accommodations. As rumors of a health hazard spread, the Sanitation Department politely asks that all visitors and residents sign a "Golden Book" by the end of May and prepare for relocation to Poland where, they are told, the climate is healthier. Doubtless, the registration spells their death. Dr. Pappenheim, the director of the summer festival, failing to comprehend the import of the brutal gestures closing in on them, reassures the inhabitants that the department simply wishes to boast of its distinguished guests and is therefore recording their names in the "Golden Book."

The mundane world of Badenheim and its simple pleasures crumble as the resort is cordoned off by sentries, mail and phone services are cut off, the hotel closes its swimming pool and does not serve food, and owners of shops are queried about the last names of their parents. That some Jews have converted—and that the majority of the protagonists are secular, deeply assimilated Jews—matters little to the Sanitation Department, which casts its nefarious net widely. The horrors unfold as a theatre of the absurd—one of the musicians describes the inspectors as "marionettes in a play,"[28] the people walk the streets "as if they were led,"[29] and the hotel waiters are later depicted as "puppets on a stage."[30] Toward the end, the city's roofs appear like "little pieces of folded cardboard."[31]

Porters deliver and unload barbed wire and cement pillars, and posters such as "THE AIR IS FRESHER IN POLAND,"[32] "LABOUR IS OUR LIFE,"[33] "SAIL ON THE VISTULA,"[34] "THE DEVELOPMENT AREAS

---

28 Ibid., 11.
29 Ibid., 25.
30 Ibid., 56.
31 Ibid., 145.
32 Ibid., 29.
33 Ibid.
34 Ibid.

NEED YOU,"³⁵ and "GET TO KNOW THE SLAVIC CULTURE"³⁶ are put up on walls, extolling the virtues of the idyllic life in Poland and inviting Polish Jews to return to their homeland and assist in building it. To compound the charade of Poland as a peaceful, pastoral destination, the office of the Sanitation Department remains open at night, slowly inveigling Jews to drop in and browse through the maps of Poland, listen to music, read through promotional leaflets and dream of their new home. This grim development is met with mixed emotion.

While everyone cooperates and heaps praise on the chilling efficiency and order displayed by the Sanitation Department, and while some are filled with pride, others are ashamed and furious. Soon, other Jews begin to arrive at Badenheim, awaiting their transfer to Poland.

Hillel Barzel argues that the town serves as the all-encompassing metaphor for the Theresienstadt Ghetto and, more broadly, the Nazi extermination process.[37] He further avers that the Holocaust, in its full dimensions, is embodied in the Sanitation Department and its actions—identification, isolation, and, finally, the liquidation of the Jews. He also asserts that those steps mirror the Nazis' comprehensive preparations for the Final Solution,[38] and astutely identifies the ironic and satiric elements that leaven the nucleus narrative:

> The absolute knowledge exhibited by the narrator is presented in contrast to the limited awareness of the protagonists who came to enjoy a summer vacation and to revel in the Festival… it is like the conventional comedy, where the spectator knows what lies behind the mask, but the heroes in the play are oblivious to the truth. In the resort town, the central character is the demonic death, responsible for setting up the annihilation process, deploying camouflage as part of its scheme. The participants in this delusion are the Jews who attempt to maintain their holiday or the continuation of their sweet existence. Had we had been watching what was being organised and its victims without the masks, we would be confronted with an atmosphere of horror.[39]

---

35   Ibid., 29–30.
36   Ibid., 30.
37   Hillel Barzel, *Ha-Me'ah ha-Ḥatsuyah: Mi-Modernizem le-Posṭ-Modernizem: Kerech 2: Monism ve-Pluralism* [*Split Century: From Modernism to Post-Modernism: Volume 2: Monism and Pluralism*] (Bnei Brak: Hakibutz Hameuchad and Sifriyat Hapoalim, 2013), 229.
38   Ibid., 237.
39   Ibid.

In examining the operative thread of Appelfeld's art, Stanley Nash maintains that the writer's fiction is "an ambivalent memorial to the generation of his murdered parents, assimilated Jews who left their seven- and eight-year old children to a hostile void of savaged nature and Gentiles" and that in Badenheim we encounter the "eerie experience of an urbane Jewish intelligentsia forcibly reunited in a common fate with the ghetto Jewry they have always shunned."[40] Indeed, as Christopher Lehmann-Haupt contends, "The town of Badenheim manages to seem all at once a gingerbread cultural center, a ghetto and one of those model concentration-camp communities that the SS prepared for inspection by the International Red Cross."[41]

One of the operating metaphors in the novel is that of the aquarium in the hotel. The fish are analogized to the isolated Jews in Badenheim and, more generally, the Jews in Nazi Europe. In one passage, the headwaiter recalls an incident that happened the year before and which directly echoes the fate of the Jews who are to be deported:

> A nature lover had brought some blue Cambium fishes and persuaded the hotel owner to put them in with the other fish. The hotel owner was a little apprehensive about the fish, but in the end, he agreed. For the first few days, the blue Cambium fish disported themselves gaily in the water, but one night they suddenly fell on the other fish and massacred them horribly. In the morning, the floor of the aquarium was full of corpses.[42]

In that connection, it is David Jacobson's contention that, in contrast to the sly machinations of the Sanitation Department that "presents its evil deeds to the victims as normal bureaucratic procedures with the purpose of benefitting the victims," the massacre of the fish is a "relatively direct portrayal of the invasion of arbitrary evil into the world of the victims."[43] Jacobson adds that the assault by one species on the other species "portrays symbolically the violent breakdown of the relationship between the assimilated Jews and the gentiles in Central Europe, which from the point of view of the Jews was so unexpected and inexplicable."[44]

---

40 Stanley Nash, "A Creative Sense of Impasse: Aharon Appelfeld's *Essays in the First Person*," Modern Hebrew Literature 7, no. 1–2 (Winter 1981–82): 56-59.
41 Christopher Lehmann-Haupt, "Badenheim 1939," *New York Times*, December 9, 1980.
42 Appelfeld, *Badenheim 1939*, 51.
43 David C. Jacobson, "'Kill your ordinary common sense and maybe you'll begin to understand': Aharon Appelfeld and the Holocaust," *AJS Review* 13, 1/2 (Spring–Autumn 1988), 150.
44 Ibid., 150.

Later, as the Jews are ordered to assemble in the train station, Karl, one of the vacationers, carries with him a bottle into which he has placed the green fish of the aquarium that have replaced the blue ones. While two are already dead, the rest are floating limply and without energy, a portent for the death from suffocation and starvation that struck the Jews transported to the killing centers in Poland.

The calm self-deceit of the residents is staggering. "They denied the existence of evil and refused to see it among others," Appelfeld has observed, "even when the monstrous wickedness was already lurking."[45] All but a very few people are overly alarmed by the claustrophobic harbingers of mounting terror. Several of the nameless holiday makers hazard guesses as to the true purpose of these regulations. Some are uneasy and nervous, "as if some alien spirit had descended."[46] As waiters serve ice cream, talk of death grows, and the Yanuka sings about the "dark forests where the wolf dwelt."[47] In an eerily prophetic conversation about deportation, one of the musicians asks his colleague why they are being sent to Poland: "'Historical necessity,' he said. 'Kill me, I don't understand. Ordinary common sense can't comprehend it.' 'In that case, kill your ordinary common sense and maybe you'll begin to understand.'"[48] Later, the twins grow taller and became emaciated, resembling the inmates of the death camps.

Most rationalize away any implications of annihilation and terror: "The festival's probably going to be a big affair this year; otherwise why would be the Sanitation Department be going to all this trouble?" Dr. Pappenheim optimistically declares.[49] In another passage, he aids and abets the Sanitation Department's chicanery: "Pappenheim would tell them about Poland. About the wonderful world to which they were going. 'Here we have no life left,' he would say. 'Here everything has become empty.'"[50] Or: "There's nothing to be afraid of… There are many Jews living in Poland. In the last analysis, a man has to return to his origins."[51] The author appeared to understand this lack of comprehension by the Jews of Badenheim when he stated that, "This world appears to be rational (with trains, departure times, stations

---

45 Aharon Appelfeld, *Beyond Despair: Three Lectures and a Conversation with Philip Roth* (New York: Fromm International, 1994), 13.
46 Appelfeld, *Badenheim 1939*, 25.
47 Ibid., 46.
48 Ibid., 70.
49 Ibid., 15.
50 Ibid., 97.
51 Ibid., 89.

and engineers), but in fact these were journeys of the imagination, lies and ruses which only deep, irrational drives could have invented."[52]

As their world begins to fall to pieces, the unnerved—but still defiantly trusting—vacationers ignore, deny, or trivialize these intrusions. As they obligingly assist the Sanitation Department, a few rationalize the ominous changes and put the best complexion on the ever-growing paper-thin fiction that they will all soon be transported to Poland. The implications of the impending catastrophe loom large in the text. How they appear, though, is set in such a way that hardly any of the characters seem aware of this, and those who are aware, few as they are, cannot convey their fears to the others.

For instance, key performers in the concert series fail to arrive; new travellers come to Badenheim as they are deported from their homes; there is a breakdown of health facilities; and food supplies and social services diminish to the point of shortages. Some vacationers storm the pharmacy in search of drugs. The Jews, who are not allowed to leave or go on excursions or picnics, become prisoners in their own resort as a sense of isolation, deprivation, and dread envelops the town, though none of the residents try to escape. In a nod to what awaits them, one of the town's dogs is shot when attempting to run away. As autumn arrives, the vacationers are incarcerated in the hotel.

Occasionally, there seem to be forebodings and intuitions of the horrors ahead, though against the grain of the text itself, they tend to be put aside by the narrator, misinterpreted by most of the characters, or simply overlooked by everyone except the critical reader. Only a few minor persons seem to realize what is actually happening, who then either try to escape or, failing that, commit suicide. The worst has virtually happened: the people in Badenheim have become mere fragments and fading memories of themselves long before they board the railway wagons that transport them to their liquidation. They have transformed into disembodied spirits—ghosts, wisps of smoke[53]—to be absorbed into the walls, furniture, and noise of their own voices.

Just before the transport takes place, Frau Zauberlit, who had escaped from a sanatorium to come to Badenheim, is rounded up by two guards and is taken to a separate transfer that has medical supervision. The reader,

---

52 Appelfeld, *Beyond Despair*, 66.
53 One of Appelfeld's early stories is entitled '*Ashan* [*Smoke*]; while the murdered victims of the Shoah were transformed into smoke by the fires of the crematoria, those who survived the horrors felt themselves to be, as the author points out, nothing but smoke as well (see Ramras-Rauch, *Aharon Appelfeld*, 51). A *holocaust* was a burnt offering from which nothing was left but smoke rising from the altar.

armed with historical knowledge, may figure that Frau Zauberlit will, in all likelihood, not be sent to Poland, but will be shot before the journey takes place, as often happened to mental patients in asylums.

Finally, by the time the assimilated Jews and half-Jews—now jumbled together, filled with restrained or outright optimism, and impatient to leave—are given the order to pack their bags and gather in an orderly fashion at the railway station, they have become less than ghosts. At this point, reality descends very quickly. As the anticlimactic ending draws closer, the train arrives in dawn to transport the Jews to their final destination of Auschwitz or Treblinka. The four freight cars into which the Jews are pushed in by the still anonymous enemy—"Get in, yelled invisible forces,"[54]—are filthy, but the sinister nature of this event is once again misread by Dr. Pappenheim, who, clutching to the familiar notions of the enlightened world, is the only one to still possess the power of speech: "If the coaches are so dirty it must mean that we have not far to go."[55] Earlier, the conductor tells one of the waitresses, "This is only a transition. Soon we'll arrive in Poland. New sights, new people. A man must broaden his horizons, no?"[56]

Even though the last words of the novel come from a figure who is guilty of a monstrous error of interpretation, the reality is no longer real because language has failed utterly. On the other hand, one critic goes against the traditional grain of analysis in contending that rather than being impaired by an "incurable self-delusion," Pappenheim's cheerful and optimistic explanation of the trains may signify the "…brave front assumed by someone who really does know just what terrible fate awaits him, for two chapters earlier the narrative unobtrusively noted the fact that Pappenheim took no luggage with him."[57]

Their doom mirrors the fate of most Jews in Europe in the 1940s. Words make no sense. They refer to nothing at all. They are neither lies, nor dreams, nor rhetorical puffs of allusion. The "facts" the narrator reports do not register on the consciousness of the characters in the fiction. As the narrative draws to an end, the Nazis succeeded in erasing any signs of uniqueness or humanity from the former vacationers, as the Jews of Badenheim are "sucked in as easily as grains of wheat poured into a funnel."[58]

---

54   Appelfeld, *Badenheim 1939*, 147.
55   Ibid., 148.
56   Ibid., 143.
57   Edward Alexander, *The Holocaust: History and the War of Ideas* (New Brunswick, NJ: Transaction Publishers, 1994), 100.
58   Appelfeld, *Badenheim 1939*, 185.

This numb acquiescence, fused with a lack of awareness by the agreeable Jews of why nothing works anymore or concern over vague, dark hints and signals that they are marked for extermination, proves to be the most disturbing part of the novel. The reason is that it resists any normative approach to the persons and events as realistic and therefore is deeply disturbing to questioning readers who have set ideas about both historical seriousness and accuracy that ought to be adhered to in Holocaust literature. In an interview with Clive Sinclair, Appelfeld shed some light on this phenomenon: "It was all too real, yet it could not be explained by the laws pertaining to the familial world. It was real but incomprehensible. The effect of this is shattering."[59]

For even the instruments of oppression and death must wait for instructions and clarifications: "The registration was over. The officials now sat in the Sanitation Department drinking tea. They had done what they had been told to do. Now they were waiting for instructions.[60] After all, when it was all over, they could say: 'I was only following orders.' It is as though moral responsibility and independent action have been snuffed out, too, and all that is left is what Hannah Arendt called "the banality of evil."[61]

A recurring motif in the narrative is the protagonists' Jewish identity and heritage, which they at first reject, then embrace. When a rabbi asks, "Are you all Jews here?"[62] his query alludes to the fact that most of those Jews are not the reviled *Ostjuden* of Eastern Europe but rather are people who consider themselves Austrian, having relegated their Jewish ancestry to the margins of their consciousness. In fact, some of the characters express their hatred of their East European kin. Most plainly, as their fall nears, the inhabitants begin admitting their discomfort with their Jewishness, as if it were "an old illness which there was no longer any point in hiding."[63] In one scene, a newcomer to the town bursts into the hotel and threatens to kill the owner: "Ostjuden, you're to blame."[64]

Yet, some of the protagonists seek comfort in the Jewish tradition and in the past they tried to bury. For example, a few of the Germanized Jews begin to learn Yiddish, such as the headwaiter who comes to believe the language is interesting. Hence, when a long forgotten, unnamed rabbi

---

59 Clive Sinclair, "ICA Guardian Conversation: Aharon Appelfeld with Clive Sinclair." Video.
60 Appelfeld, *Badenheim 1939*, 71.
61 Hannah Arendt, *Eichmann in Jerusalem: A Report on the Banality of Evil* (New York: Viking, 1963).
62 Appelfeld, *Badenheim 1939*, 101.
63 Ibid., 21.
64 Ibid., 99.

appears among the guests and staff in Badenheim to join the deportees, he is immediately welcomed as the town's spiritual leader. Indeed, the guests insist on taking the once-banished old man along with them on the death train, pushing his wheelchair to the station. This group of people, who for the most part thought they had jettisoned all their past commitments to Judaism and its beliefs and who are now in a state of shocked denial to find themselves requested to register as Jews in order to facilitate their forced transfer to Poland, are gripped by utter confusion when this figure of traditional knowledge and authority tries to speak to them. The rabbi is himself barely aware of why they suddenly cry aloud to him for help and guidance:

> The rabbi woke from his slumbers and said aloud, "What do they want." All these years they haven't paid any attention to the Torah. Me they locked away in an old-age home. They didn't want to have anything to do with me. Now they want to go to Poland. There is no atonement without asking forgiveness first.[65]

When the rabbi talks, it is "in a jumble of Hebrew and Yiddish"[66] and makes no sense to them. Even were it in German, which they think they can still understand, his words do not address their needs, and none can connect with the causes of the present, increasingly overwhelming crisis. For it is no more a matter of atonement for sins that is required to set things right in the world again than it is for these people to file petitions, send in letters asking for rectifications of policies, or anything having to do with logic or reason: "The sceptical bitterness did not leave the rabbi's lips. He placed no faith in these delusions. He had seen much in his life and all that was left in him was suspicion, and in this transition too his suspicions did not cease but only grew more intense."[67]

If the rabbi is serious here, then he must be crazy, since he had actually seen very little that can explain what is going on. If he is not serious, but only making jokes, his cynical, sceptical wit goes beyond nonsense to deconstruct all pretentiousness. Whereas the awakened rabbi's bitterness undermines his effectiveness as a teacher and guide, it is not because Judaism and its history have failed to provide a way of surviving the Holocaust. Rather, it is because the Shoah is unprecedented and resists all explanations, rationalizations, or theosophies. It is an enigma wrapped up in a mystery.

---

65   Ibid., 143.
66   Ibid., 143.
67   Ibid., 145.

The characters of Appelfeld's novel no longer belong to a world in which logic, narrative direction, or human relationships exist. They are already dead and forgotten. By then, the outside towns and cities of Austria—like those in the Third Reich and the conquered territories—were rapidly becoming *Jüdenrein*, and all that was once identified as Jewish culture in Europe had passed into "oblivion." On the one hand, the world of *Yiddishkeit* remains a vague memory and a slight tinge of nostalgia, while on the other hand, the supposedly modern culture of assimilation has begun to crumble away between their fingers. That vague memory itself draws into itself and hides—in the modern Hebrew that Appelfeld writes—"a hallucinatory quality"[68] of all that otherwise cannot be expressed in words—in rhythms of speech, in silence between syntactical and grammatical sequences, and in figures of speech transmogrified into Israeli Hebrew when characters dream, rationalize, or deny what they see and feel.

Similarly, another one of these traditional carnival masks—the pedantic fool, Professor Fussholdt—roused from his own intellectual stupor, provides no help either. This erudite scholar who spends the summer proofreading his *magnum opus*, the topic of which is never disclosed, tries to provide a foothold in the words he uses to connect them to the current reality. But his speech parodies not only the rabbinic commentators and moralists of the sacred text or the assimilated agents for the supposedly secular and tolerant modern state, but also any Jewish language: "Professor Fussholdt imitated the rhetoric of the Jewish functionaries who imagined that they were bringing the Messiah with their speeches."[69]

Yet, in the very act of losing himself in his pedantic writings, he has softened his attitudes toward the very art and culture, as well as religion, that he previously spurned. Now, instead of pompous silence, he babbles in bombastic noise:

> His hostility to everything considered Jewish culture, Jewish art, was lighter now. The bitterness and mockery had been buried in his book. Mitzi [Frau Fussholdt] walked behind him like a stranger. The longer they walked the more his eloquence flowed, full of ingenious puns, witticisms, and plays on words. For months he had not spoken to a soul and now the words poured out of him.[70]

---

68 James Hatley, "Impossible Mourning: Two Attempts to Remember Annihilation," *The Centennial Review* 35, no. 3 (1991): 446.
69 Appelfeld, *Badenheim 1939*, 140–41.
70 Ibid., 141.

Another of the predominant themes to emerge in the novel is sickness and madness. The deranged mind of the recently released mental patient, Trude, the pharmacist's wife, can be still heard in her voice, stemming from "her hallucinations."[71] Those aberrations are the embodiment of the madness within herself that she has brought back to Badenheim after her stay in a nearby sanatorium. Terminally ill, she is the only character who sees things clearly, imagining the people who returned to Badenheim, "not like the familiar vacationers, but like patients in a sanatorium."[72] Later, "Everything looked transparent and diseased to her…she was haunted by a hidden fear."[73]

Able to prophesize, she has visions of her daughter Helena as being held "captive and abused"[74] at the hands of her gentile husband. In the end, her daughter Helena does return to Badenheim, after being turned out by her non-Jewish husband. Ultimately, Trude's acute ability to foretell the horrors is proven true. Though her husband Martin at first discounts his wife's feverish delirium and hallucinations about death, as the novel ends, he no longer doubts her perceptiveness: "He too began to see patches of paleness on people's faces…Martin felt that he was becoming infected with her hallucinations."[75] Her diseased mind at once reflects the spiritual and physical disintegration of the inhabitants of Badenheim, as well as the warped policies and actions of the Third Reich.

In one passage, we read that, "Martin felt that he was becoming infected by her hallucinations."[76] Thus, Martin and everyone else in the town are polluted by her crazy dreams. Indeed, all the people in Badenheim are now living in a madhouse, or at least somewhere that is no longer attached to logic, truth, or reality. In a sense, all of the Jews of Austria who did not run away before or just after the Anschluss are mad, and are treated as the sewage that is flooding the one-real town of Badenheim. They are therefore effluence to be flushed into the Nazi sewage system that is the Holocaust.

In *Badenheim 1939*, the closest to a character narrator or protagonist is Dr. Pappenheim, the impresario in charge of organizing the musical festival that brings visitors to the town during the holiday season. He is therefore the man to whom most of the townsfolk and visitors turn to for advice on how to interpret the delays in the arrival of guest performers and regular

---

71   Ibid., 3.
72   Ibid., 3.
73   Ibid., 3, 10.
74   Ibid., 3.
75   Ibid., 4, 11.
76   Ibid., 11.

musicians, causing frustration and disappointments in the smooth workings of the entertainment services provided. Everyone also complains to him about the unavailability of sufficient food and medicine, and express their doubts as to the success of the season. It is in conversations with him that they reveal their niggling fears that crop up over rumors of malevolent events back in Vienna or closer to town in the forests and country villages. Though most of the residents sense the approaching monstrosity without being able to grasp its complete dimensions, Dr. Pappenheim attempts to assuage their worries, not because he is an inveterate optimist but rather because he feels it is his duty to cheer them up.

He is certain that the new sights and new people in Poland that await the inhabitants of Badenheim will be stimulating. He himself has doubts and anxieties, like the rest. He does not express them both because he hopes for the best, which is not the same thing as denying that there are problems, and because his understanding of the larger picture is rather limited. Because of these deficiencies in his character, Pappenheim's fatuous rationalizations are more than merely the misconstructions of a pompous fool who is meant to represent a whole class of assimilated Austrian Jews unable to read the clues and who are marched off "like sheep to the slaughter."

In Appelfeld, we encounter the inadequacy of language to portray the terror of the Shoah, including the Hebrew that Appelfeld uses to inscribe his essays, stories, and novels. Whether they were too young to have words to express what they went through or have been traumatized by the experience, Appelfeld's narrators tend to be people without language, either physically mute or nearly so ("spare and distant," as Tamar Drukker puts it)[77] or they are in some way emotionally or psychologically disturbed (creating those distances between the mature self and the alienated other caused by trauma).[78]

In *Badenheim 1939*, the narrator and the fictional characters are for the most part not children, although there is one Yiddish-speaking *Wunderkind* or child prodigy, Nahum Slotzker, and one madwoman, Trude, who speaks in the visionary terms of her dreams. Despite these exceptions of a boy genius and a lunatic, what is spoken in the novel or even what the characters imagine that they hear from the new regime invading their holiday resort is silence. Drukker thus cites Jeffrey M. Green, a man who has translated many of Appelfeld's Hebrew works, who describes Appelfeld's use of language as a tool to express something that is known and experienced before

---

77   Tamar S. Drukker, "Language and Silences in two of Aharon Appelfeld's Coming-of-Age Tales," *Yod* 19 (2014): 3.
78   Ibid.

or beyond language. Language trails behind the meaning and essence rather than creating and defining them.⁷⁹

This is the great paradox of *Badenheim 1939*. It is an artistically crafted literary text whose main fiction is that is written in a language that can neither be heard, spoken, nor read because it is invalid, inadequate—and constantly fading away into pure silence, "…and the silence, the loaded silence that kept the people apart…."⁸⁰ During an interview with Yad Vashem, Appelfeld said, "…just as the Jew's every fibre leaned toward assimilation, there came a radical satanic force that not only halted this trend but wiped out the people who were inclined to pursue this process. That's the tragedy of the Holocaust."⁸¹ In *Badenheim 1939*, there is no tragedy because that ancient genre requires awareness, struggle, or resistance to fate; instead, the characters in the novel are already oblivious, caught in a nightmare they do not know they are dreaming, and belong to the dead before they board the transports to Auschwitz and other death camps.

Though the characters in the novel generally assume that their assimilation into Austro-Germanic culture has been successful and that they form a constituent part of the general population in these sophisticated lands—especially in Vienna, where they tend to live in their supposedly normal lives—the truth is somewhat different. This truth forms one of the keys to the way the novel is composed and received.⁸² In Appelfeld's novel, the transformation of German from a sophisticated modern European language into an ugly tissue of distortions and lies is taken several steps further. Thus, the poignant illusion of the Hebrew text in its pretence to be in German is that the speakers cannot only not say or think anything true about themselves or the impending disaster looming over them, but actually cannot see what is going on. Their conversations and inner thoughts rendered by the narrator are nothing but a web of lies, self-deceptions, and grotesque distortions of reality. However, it had been related to experience and feelings in the past—that is, formally until the day of *Anschluss* on March 12, 1938—once Austria disappears into the *Third Reich*, it is totally impossible for them to deal with reality. They are locked into a pocket of unreality and delusions.

At the same time—yet already evident in Germany as the National Socialist revolution takes place in political, social, and legal terms—the

---

79 Ibid., 6.
80 Appelfeld, *Badenheim 1939*, 94.
81 Amos Goldberg and Amos T., "An Interview with the Author Prof. Aharon Appelfeld," *Shoah Resource Center* (January 25, 1988): 2.
82 Ibid., 6.

nature of German as a respectable language of culture, science, and philosophy transforms into a bundle of canards and fabrications. From Hitler's speeches through an endless series of decrees, to ordinary commercial transactions, everyday slang and domestic speech, nothing truthful or respectable can be spoken. This can be seen in the functioning of the agencies of the Nazi regime emblemized in the Sanitation Department, the advertisements for holidays and resettlement in Poland, and the provision of healthcare and other civil activities. The characters in *Badenheim 1939* do not discern the discrepancies between what they had previously known and wanted to believe about their own Jewish past in Poland's cities, *shtetls*, and religious communities. They have already lost any standards or procedures for thinking. This too is part of the genocide that precedes the implementation of the *Enlösung*. It is not because they are wilfully oblivious and culpable in their own destruction as individuals or a community; in the resort village of Badenheim, they are already prisoners, worn down to *Musselmänner* (the walking dead), already dead and forgotten. The town of Badenheim is in this way already outside of history, and the people, caught up within its barbed-wire barriers, are no longer real. They are shadows on the wall speaking the lies of the past and the mirage of the unreal present or, as Gila Ramras-Rauch put it, "hovering shadows of an extinct reality."[83]

Badenheim 1939 has been called satire, with the sense that it privileges a criticism of the assimilated Jews (those who believe they have sloughed off their old skins of the *Ostjüden* and become "Austrian citizens of Jewish origin"[84]) who allowed themselves through self-deception to fall victim to events that they should have attempted to avoid by any means possible. From this perspective, the characters in the novel are found culpable of colluding with their own destruction, if not in the last fatal moments before the iron gate falls to shut them off from rescue, then at least in the decades before the rise of Nazi ideology. In those years, they fooled themselves into believing they could assimilate more or less fully into the surrounding society, which they took to be tolerant, welcoming, and even at times respectful of their contributions to its economy, culture, and social milieu. They are blamed for leaving behind not just their communities and families, but their own forms of knowledge and reasoning, disconnecting themselves from their entire history. According to this school of thought, they are little better than the *Judenrat* and *kapos* who collaborated with the Nazis in running the death factories of the Holocaust. Particularly in the eyes of the *sabra* (native-born Israelis), these European Jewish victims were seen

---

83 Ramras-Rauch, *Aharon Appelfeld*, 51.
84 Appelfeld, *Badenheim 1939*, 21.

to have been led like sheep to the slaughter. However, even a casual glance at Appelfeld's fiction shows that there is no such satiric intent in his work.

Michael Bernstéin—in his book, *Foregone Conclusions: Against Apocalyptic History*[85]—launches a blistering attack on Appelfeld, excoriating the author for crafting individuals who remain achingly and naïvely oblivious to their nearing doom. This follows an earlier highly critical essay by Ruth Wisse, in which she argues that in his writings Appelfeld projects the anger he feels towards his parents onto his figures and, as such, "Fate sits in judgment on all the ugly, assimilated Jews—fate in the form of the Holocaust. The result is a series of pitiless moral fables, more damning of the victims than of the crime committed against them."[86] Appelfeld expressed his shock upon reading the critique: "She said some terrible things: that my writing is filled with self-hatred and hatred of Jews. I couldn't believe it when I read it. She writes that I condemn the victims. The *victims*! A vicious article!"[87]

For his part, Bernstéin accuses Appelfeld of manipulating the literary device of backshadowing, and forcefully maintains that Appelfeld treats his heroes as "marionettes whose futile gestures on an absurd stage we watch, half in horror, half in anxiously bemused melancholy."[88] According to Bernstéin, Appelfeld is guilty of being as "moralistic and judgemental as the sternest critic of Austro-German Jewry, and just as with all backshadowing perspectives, its termination in the abyss of the Shoah is adduced to 'prove' the meaninglessness of Jewish life in Aryan Europe."[89] Bernstéin goes even further in his harsh denouncement, claiming that Appelfeld's stylistic method and approach in *Badenheim 1939* not only thrust the subject of responsibility for the extermination of the Jews into the foreground, but questions it. In Bernstéin's view, Appelfeld, "by representing the Jews of Badenheim as irredeemably selfish and petty…commits the greater offense of leaving unchallenged the monstrous proposition that Europe's Jews are somehow 'deserving' of punishment."[90]

While embracing a less accusatory tone toward the author, Avidov Lipsker and Avi Sagi nevertheless traverse a similar terrain to Bernstein. They maintain that the unique element to be uncovered in Appelfeld's

---

[85] Michael Andre Bernstéin, *Foregone Conclusions: Against Apocalyptic History* (Berkeley, CA: University of California Press, 1994).
[86] Ruth Wisse, "Aharon Appelfeld, Survivor," *Commentary*, August 1, 1983: 76.
[87] Haim Chertok, *We are All Close: Conversations with Israeli Writers* (New York: Fordham University Press, 1989), 23.
[88] Bernstéin, *Foregone Conclusions*, 58.
[89] Ibid., 61–62.
[90] Ibid., 66.

thematic matrix is an unusually uncommon response to one of the most painful and challenging quandaries about the Holocaust—the great Nazi fraud or deception of their victims. While the historical hypothesis ventured, Lipsker and Sagi argue, namely the demonic cunning of the perpetrators, Appelfeld anchors his explanation in the "mentality of the victims and their mental state, which always lead them to deceive themselves, absent of any causal relation to their objective situation."[91]

Bernstéin's study of *Badenheim 1939* demonstrates the dangers of taking literally and historically a fictive text that does not seek to represent a faithful delineation of Jewish life in Austria after the German absorption of the nation into a new Nazi empire. Set against what actually transpired among Jews once their inevitable fate became evident, the characters in Appelfeld's novel can be taken as demented fools, self-deluded sleepwalkers, or misplaced characters out of a turn-of-the-century farce portrayed in all the clichés and jokes of the genre. If the assimilated Jews who gather in Badenheim in late summer 1939 to attend a music festival as usual—and the others who arrive because they are forced to assemble in preparation for deportation to Poland and eventual extermination in death camps—were so utterly unaware of reality, they would indeed be not only the "sheep going quietly to the slaughter" as some Zionist propagandists would have it, but also to a certain degree morally responsible for their own fate. They would also bear the blame of not understanding how cutting themselves off from traditional rabbinic values and practices left them with no spiritual or psychological resources with which to meet their fate with dignity and spiritual calm. In that connection, one feels hard pressed not to cite Alexander, who in taking issue with Bernstéin's operating thesis, notes that "only a foolishly self-confident reader will conclude that he, in the same circumstances, would have acted better, more wisely, more bravely, than Pappenheim and the other doomed Jews."[92]

But though Bernstéin recognizes to some degree that Appelfeld's book has satirical and allegorical dimensions, he does not accept these mitigating generic circumstances as sufficient to excuse the novelist from either trivializing the horrors of the Shoah or failing to grasp the responsibilities of an artist to respect the woeful dimensions of so many victims and survivors. He is unable to reconcile the two options he sets out. On the one hand,

---

91 Avidov Lipsker and Avi Sagi. "Through an Icy Corridor to the Roots of Jewish Identity," in *Twenty-Four Readings in Aharon Appelfeld's Literary Work*, ed. Lipsker Avidov and Avi Sagi (Ramat Gan: Bar Ilan University Press and Shalom Hartman Institute, 2011), 10.

92 Alexander, *The Holocaust*, 100.

he suggests that Badenheim, place and narrative, is "a typical Austrian spa town"[93] and a "microcosm of the world of Austro-German Jewry with its cultural pretensions."[94] On the other hand, he suggests that what happens there is "hallucinatory," an "absurd" and "fable-like" distortion of reality.[95] Bernstéin can also grant the novelist an intention to generate various ironies that were confected for the Israeli reader (Appelfeld's original audience since the book was published in Hebrew) who were expected to recognize discrepancies between how the action is described and the way visitors to the spa interpret disturbances to their normal experiences and news from outside. Obviously enough, at the time of publication, Israeli readers would have been pleased at their own superior knowledge, angry at the perverse refusal to see what is patent, and satisfied with their own lives in a Jewish state. Contra Bernstéin, Emily Miller Budick maintains that *Badenheim 1939*

> ...does not need the correction afforded by sideshadowing. It is not the novel's primary purpose to mount a cultural critique or even to distribute blame on one or both sides of the catastrophe. Rather, the text captures a psychological, emotional moment on the part of the narrative voice that happens to be, we know, a survivor's...He does not...imagine that the present enables us to understand and thereby free ourselves from the past. Instead he recognises the impossibility of responding to the past without entering into a meaningful, even passionate relationship with it.[96]

Likewise, David Hirsh contends that if "Bernstein had been able to get beyond his theory he would have seen that Appelfeld portrays with great artistry what Bernstein himself has described as the 'pervasive terror that gripped Austrian Jewry within hours of the Anschluss.'"[97]

Bernstéin also asserts that readers of the novel will feel shock at this inconsistency and holds Appelfeld to account for lacking sympathy at the plight of those foolish Jews in Europe who tried to argue themselves into total passivity in the face of evil. Such a supposed audience would also tend to side with Hannah Arendt's version of the Holocaust as she propounded it in *Eichmann in Jerusalem*, wherein she turned the Nazi arch-murderer into a "banal" bureaucrat merely following orders and characterized Israelis

---

93 Bernstéin, *Foregone Conclusions*, 59.
94 Ibid.
95 Ibid.
96 Emily Miller Buddick, *Aharon Appelfeld's Fiction: Acknowledging the Holocaust* (Bloomington: Indiana University Press, 2005), 230, 231.
97 David Hirsch, "Review of *Foregone Conclusions: Against Apocalyptic History*," *Criticism* 37, no. 2 (Spring 1995): 335.

as vengeful hypocrites pursuing him outside of natural and existing positive law merely to conduct a "show trial."[98] By wishing to try Eichmann for crimes against the Jewish People, Arendt argued, the authorities in Jerusalem were no better than the Nazis who sought to exclude Jews from the category of the human, as the Allied Nuremberg Trials attempted to do immediately after World War II with a new category of "Crimes against Humanity." Thus, Appelfeld himself is held morally culpable of literary minimization and even an ethical lack of responsibility to the dead and the survivors of the Holocaust. The novel, in other words, is bereft of authenticity, insight, and sympathy.

To be sure, there is the predictable and natural urge to condemn and judge the Jews of Badenheim for their inaction, their self-delusion, and their refusal to see the noose tightening around their necks for what it really was. A better approach, as we have tried to show, would see *Badenheim 1939* as a novel in which the existential realities and normal language of pre-*Anschluss* Austria have already lost their validity and are, like the people, caught up in the historical fate of the Holocaust—fading away into emptiness, oblivion, and desolate memories. Tattered fragments of what was once true set in a mesh of inadequate and false language, the fictional text screams out for renewal, a renewal with a more sensible and knowledgeable understanding of Jewish history, culture, and theology. It is as wrong to blame the victims as it is to absolve the victimizers, and as meaningless to try to write in the barbaric way of Holocaust deniers, postmodernist relativism, and simplistic religious paradigms.

In a wide-ranging conversation with Philip Roth, who considers Appelfeld to be "fiction's foremost chronicler of the Holocaust,"[99] the Israeli novelist furnishes the readers with an instructive elucidation on the thematic template that undergirds *Badenheim 1939* and his artistic motivations in how he framed the story. Though not directly, Appelfeld addresses Bernstéin's criticism in the following:

> In *Badenheim 1939* I completely ignored the historical explanation. I assumed that the historical facts were known to the readers and that they would fill in what was missing…I was a victim, and I try to understand the victim. That is a broad, complicated expanse of life that I've been trying to deal with for 30 years now. I haven't idealized the victims. I don't think that in "Badenheim

---

98 Arendt. *Eichmann in Jerusalem*, 1963, 4.
99 Tonkin Boyd, "How Aharon Appelfeld Chronicled the Holocaust," *The Independent*, May 19, 2012, accessed August 8, 2018, https://www.independent.co.uk/arts-entertainment/books/features/how-aharon-appelfeld-chronicled-the-holocaust-7763595.html.

1939" there's any idealization either…It is generally agreed, to this day, that Jews are deft, cunning and sophisticated creatures, with the wisdom of the world stored in them. But isn't it fascinating to see how easy it was to fool the Jews? With the simplest, almost childish tricks they were gathered up in ghettos, starved for months, encouraged with false hopes and finally sent to the death by train. That ingenuousness stood before eyes while I was writing "Badenheim." In that ingenuousness, I found a kind of distillation of humanity. Their blindness and deafness, their obsessive preoccupation with themselves is an integral part of their ingenuousness. The murderers were practical, and they knew just what they wanted. The ingenuous person is always a shlimazl, a clownish victim of misfortune, never hearing the danger signals in time, getting mixed up, tangled up and finally falling in the trap. Those weaknesses charmed me. I fell in love with them… Fate was already hidden within those people like a mortal illness. Assimilated Jews built a structure of humanistic values and looked out on the world from it. They were certain they were no longer Jews, and that what applied to "the Jews" did not apply to them. That strange assurance made them into blind or half-blind creatures. I have always loved assimilated Jews, because that was where the Jewish character, and also, perhaps, Jewish fate, was concentrated with greatest force.[100]

In a wide-ranging interview with Schmuel Schneider, Appelfeld described the staggering self-delusion that gripped Polish Jews, mirroring the lack of perception of the characters in Badenheim. He explained that when the Germans invaded Czernowitz in August 1940, and the Russians withdrew, the townsfolk rejoiced at their arrival. Though hard to accept, Appelfeld notes, they believed that this episode was one of momentary madness, and that they were safe in the hands of a cultured nation, "A Jewish Anschluss…one has to understand that the German-Jewish symbiosis is very deep, without a precedent in Jewish culture. It was sheer insanity, hypnosis. It took a long time for the realisation to descend that they were murderers. After all, Germans are associated with literature, theatre, music—everything that is enlightened."[101]

Other critics have tried to understand Appelfeld's stories as parables and allegories, as though the persons, places, and actions in the fiction had little or no significance in themselves but stood in the place of something else, an argument—not necessarily satirical—but more abstract, theoretical, and philosophical. As such, each narrative, in this sense, would represent some

---
100 Appelfeld, *Beyond Despair*, 84.
101 Schneider, *Existence and Memory*, 101.

moral or spiritual lesson to be learned, a cautionary tale, a revealed meaning in bravery or failure to be strong. The parable strips down an event to a few brief actions, the characters to a small number of exemplary types, and the setting to a simple paradigmatic situation that clarifies complex issues. In allegory, even further, the constituent elements of the narrative are shaped around an external and logical argument, in which what happened is less central than why it happened. Again, Appelfeld's body of work does not lend itself to this sort of exposition: his persons, experiences, and ordeals are set in a world sans logic or meaning, and where no one can escape one's destiny because there is no providential or demonic order—only madness and undeserved death.

In *Badenheim 1939*, the very opposite conditions seem to be evident. Though set in a dark and ominous forest, where unseen and unheard dangers press in upon the visitors to the resort, there is no confrontation let alone an attempt to flee or hide away in disguise. At best, some of the nice people try to explain away any hints of the evil that lurks and then begins to pounce. Like Kafka's protagonists, the visiting Jews identify with power and authority, as though the absurd decrees were rational regulations and the horrible changes to their lives proof of better things to come.

Nothing follows from what precedes or leads anywhere other than to what the ancients called an *aporia*, a point beyond which logic cannot go. While the spring season returns to Badenheim, it is a period (not necessarily of time but of experience and apprehension) of transition. Therefore, the progress of the seasons marks a change in its inhabitants, yet the focus is not clear, whether it is the movement of light that retreats or sewage that flows. The church out in the forest near the resort town rings, but why is unclear: it could be to welcome a new beginning, mourn a terrible loss, or merely to register the flow of time in its natural order. There are many inferences to be drawn, but not all are actually implied in that sequence or in the whole narrative text that forms the novel. When the shadows of the forest retreat to the trees, this could be a fanciful way of stating that the sun illuminated the scene or day replaced night, the remnants of whose darkness could still be perceived until then. Or it could mean that the shadows disappeared into and sought shelter in the trees, a retreat consequent to the invasion by vacationers, the holiday-makers who come every year but not always the same individuals, or at this particular time are different as well because those who return have a different motivation and the new guests have been forced to leave their homes in the unseen city.

The seasonal and natural movement of the sentences, when the transition is about to begin, is not yet clear or evident. The shift then comes from the external setting to the inner events in progress, the invasion of the inspectors who examine the flow of sewage in the pipes hidden from normal view. Note that the sewage flows in only, not in and out of the pipes. This is a closed system, with ominous implications in the very nature of the waste circulating through the town, all seeming to culminate in the designation of the town's beauty as modest. This does not come as a natural conclusion to what has been said throughout the paragraph, even if we take *modest* in its least ambiguous sense as nonboastful rather than morally upright and socially shy.

James Hatley suggests that Appelfeld assumes readers of *Badenheim 1939* will bring to the novel their own experiences as survivors, children, or friends of those who endured the worst of the worst, or at least persons who have read and studied the Holocaust so that they are constantly measuring the gaps, voicing the silences, and interpreting the perplexing text in the light of what is beyond words and images in the novel.[102] To a certain degree, this is certainly true; thus, the book would demand close and interactive attention from its audience. But this process of reader participation would have an epistemological assumption not valid for Appelfeld's fiction: it would mean that there was somewhere a logical, coherent, truthful historical argument of the Shoah. It would mean that the void left by all those who died and left no memory at all could be filled in. This seems precisely what the author denies. For him, language has failed, as has culture and religion, and only a visceral yet silent and invisible injury remains. "The dead of Auschwitz," Hatley almost rightly avers, "even more than the dead of more normal times, sink into a past from which they cannot return and so trouble those who mourn, those who remain after to ponder the dead."[103] While the words *invasion* and *retreat* seem in retrospect to allude to some political-military event—such as the entrance of German troops into Austria on the day of *Anschluss*—the structure of the imagery only allows the reader to see the arrival of spring, the coming of dawn, and a flood of daylight replacing the retreating shadows. What has changed, then, is the arrival of the summer visitors and the seemingly orderly civil engineers of the sewage pipes to ensure the health of the town's population, two

---

102 Hatley, "Impossible Mourning," 450. A similar rationalization is mounted by Thelma Bryant in her review of *Badenheim 1939* (Thelma Bryant, "*Badenheim 1939* by Appelfeld," *The San Francisco Jung Institute Library Journal* 2, no. 3 [1981]: 39–41). Yet, in addition to her Jungian psychoanalytic terms of reference, in which she attempts to link Appelfeld's novel to various folkloric and literary genres—tragedy, parable, and the like—she finds "the language is so fluid, fluent, economical that I believe this [translation] must be a faithful rendition of the author's intention" (p. 39).
103 Hatley, "Impossible Mourning," 451.

events that do not exactly square with one another since the population is on the verge of being other than it usually is and the proper (clean, as well as orderly) state of the sanitary facilities is in doubt.

It seems as though consequences precede causes, and reactions emerge before there are things to respond to. We as readers know that what is really happening to cause the village to be shut down—the inhabitants to be registered for deportation, and the cruelty inflicted on them—is part of a grotesque and diabolical master plan. However, that cannot be attached to what these people see, hear, and feel as they gradually disappear from history. In brief, while there is something like plot development by tracing the passage of time it takes for the Sanitation Department to infiltrate Badenheim and cause each of its inhabitants and visitors to register as Jews and deal in their own specific—and eccentric—way with the impending transport to Poland, the real advances in meaning throughout the novel occur sporadically as the metaphors of light and shadow form themselves into the *conceit* (ingenious and complex emblem) of death overtaking everyone and everything. Death means, however, less the loss of life through some violent act than the disintegration of intellect and consciousness. If at one point the laughter of the visitors sounds like "the breaking of delicate glass,"[104] not only does that allude to *Kristallnacht* (The Night of the Broken Glass, November 9, 1938) that erupted throughout Germany and Austria as the most ominous warning of more horrific occurrences to come, at another point it is in a more involute manner: "The people are silently absorbed in their little pleasure. Flakes of darkness now filled the corners of the room, and the space grew more confined."[105]

As for the "flakes of darkness," they can be understood as the burnt fragments of the synagogues attacked on *Kristallnacht* as well as the burnt parchment of Torah in rabbinic legends of ancient persecutions, out of which the sacred letters in flames rose to heaven like the souls of the holy martyrs ascending to Paradise. These "flakes of darkness" are also the broken husks of the vessels in which divine energy was scattered throughout the created universe, in which still hide the sparks on the other side (the *sitra achra*). At the same time, within the same words and phrases, here hidden from the figures of the narrative, the *tsimtsum* (Great Contraction of the Divine Mind to generate space and time for things to come into being) is transmuted into the very literal "concentration camps" to which Jews are "confined" on their way to the gas chambers and other methods of annihilation.

---

104 Appelfeld, *Badenheim 1939*, 56.
105 Ibid., 57.

Chapter 2

Our Mother Eve on a Death Train

Dan Pagis has been hailed as "…one of the most prominent Holocaust poets who ever wrote in the Hebrew language…His lucid, not-melodramatic tone reflects his attempts to transcend horror through the clarity of images. A purity engulfs his poetry, largely as a result of its ultimate attempt not to obfuscate language."[1] Born in Radauiti in German-speaking Bukovina, Romania, in 1930, Dan Pagis's father came from Yiddish-speaking Czernowitz and was also fluent in Russian and Romanian. However, before the newborn could begin to learn those languages at home, his father departed for Palestine and planned to bring his wife, Judith Auslander, and child there as soon as he was able. That hope did not materialize. In 1934, Dan's mother died, leaving her four-year-old son in the care of her parents. The boy was then brought up speaking German, the language he almost totally abjured once he arrived in Israel.[2]

This lonely and highly intellectual lifestyle was brought to an abrupt halt in 1941 when the Soviet Union was invaded by the German Army and the eleven-year-old Pagis was rounded up by the Nazis and transported to Transnistria, along with his maternal grandparents. While the older people were murdered in the death camps, somehow the teenager made his escape from a forced-labor battalion in 1944. Two years later, when he was sixteen, he made the perilous journey to Palestine, arriving in 1946.[3] At that time, he was able to meet his father, who had by then remarried and

---
1 Gila Ramras-Rauch, "Dan Pagis," in *Encyclopedia of Holocaust Literature*, ed. David Patterson, Alan L. Berger, and Sarita Cargas (Westport, CT: Oryx Press, 2002), 145.
2 In his last years, he began to make notes on his manuscript in German. This mother tongue must therefore have always been lying dormant.
3 At some point, after arriving in Israel and deciding not to speak German any longer, once he had mastered Hebrew, Pagis changed his forename from the German-sounding name he was given at birth, though what it is we have never learned.

was living in a small apartment in Tel Aviv. This new existence with his father and second wife proved problematic, and the young man was sent to stay in kibbutz Merhavia, a shelter for refugee children in the Yizrael Valley. While teaching in the kibbutz, he met several influential artists, such as the poets Tuvia Ruebner and Leah Goldberg, who guided his ambitions towards writing fiction in Hebrew but also encouraged him to attend university. The relationship with these two authors was pivotal to Pagis's evolution as a poet. Like his contemporaries Yehuda Amichai and Dahlia Ravikovitch, Pagis was mentored by Goldberg, who helped the young man publish his poems in the daily newspaper '*Al ha-Mishmar* and the literary journal *Orlogin*. Appositely, Michael Gluzman remarks that prior to meeting Goldberg, Pagis strove to conjure an impersonal persona in his poetry, an approach that Goldberg quickly dismissed. This is how Pagis recalls his initial encounter with Goldberg, "…I was urged to read her poetry and to show a few of my poems to Leah Goldberg. I made an appointment with her at a café and she went through my poems and said, 'I don't understand who you are. You possess insights into poetry, but what about Hebrew?' She asked about my background, and when I told her, she understood, and asserted, that in the entire pile, there were only two poems."[4] After Goldberg's death in 1970, Pagis helped Ruebner edit her collection of writings and translation of foreign poets.

Ruebner, in fact, dedicates the poem "A Farewell to a Friend" to Pagis.[5] According to Gluzman, Goldberg's remarks to Pagis represent at once an intuitive and incisive assessment of a fundamental ingredient in Pagis's poems that was already operating in his early work, namely, his determination to engage in a non-biographical and non-confessional dialogue with the reader in his writing.[6] Furthermore, Gluzman maintains that *Katuv b-'Ipparon ba-Qaron ha-Chatum* (*Written in Pencil in the Sealed Railway Car*)—the subject of this essay—embodies Pagis's resistance to employing the confessional-biographical mode in depicting the Holocaust.

Pagis's first poems appeared in 1949 in the newspaper '*Al ha-Mishmar* and his debut volume of poetry *Sha'on ha-Tzel* (*The Shadow Dial*) was published in 1959. He eventually earned a PhD at the Hebrew University of Jerusalem, where he subsequently became a Professor of Medieval Hebrew

---

4   Michael Gluzman, "Memory without a Subject: About Dan Pagis and the Poetry of the State Generation" (paper delivered at Stanford University symposium in memory of Professor Yosef Haefrati, June 17, 2007).
5   Ruth Lauper, "Ha-Dmama 'Eina Horeshet Ra'" [The Silence Plots no Evil], *Haaretz*, February 23, 2003.
6   Gluzman, "Memory without a Subject," 14.

Literature and taught there until his untimely death from cancer in 1986, at just fifty years old. It did not take Pagis long to learn Hebrew, a new language he quickly adopted for his poetic endeavors, jettisoning the German tongue and its attendant associations: "…the fact remains that his life as a poet began with a conscious decision to express himself in Hebrew rather than in his native German."[7] Not surprisingly, he struggled to find the appropriate language to express the sheer horrors of the Holocaust, choosing instead to inject his authorial voice into archetypal characters such as Eve, Cain, Abel, the victims and perpetrators. For the rest of his years, Pagis published five volumes of Hebrew verse.

Notably, Pagis never spoke about the Holocaust terrors he witnessed and experienced. His wife, Ada, in her 1995 book *Lev Pitomi* (*A Sudden Heart*) remarked that her husband, "…did not agree to talk about the expulsion. What he went through during that transfer embittered his entire life, and with all his energies he tried to conceal it from himself and from others."[8]

The six-line, minimalist poem *Katuv b-'Ipparon ba-Qaron ha-Chatum*[9] (hereinafter referred to as *Written in Pencil in the Sealed Railway Car*) remains Pagis's best known work and the most anthologized. Over the years, it has assumed an iconic, almost scriptural authority, canonized when it was inscribed on an actual railway car in Yad Vashem's "Memorial to the Deportees." Published in his third volume *Gilgul* (*Transformation*) in 1970, the original Hebrew version of this very short poem is cryptic and suggestive. It implies a specific scene in which the words were first penned, and a number of possible rhetorical contexts in which the document is found, read, and interpreted by different kinds of readers—or even no readers at all. A Pandora's box of ambiguous meanings and layers, it melds the familiar mythical narrative with the twentieth century's darkest chapter to produce a historical and literary artifact that reaches beyond the anguished and temporal life of one Jewish woman and her son to transcendent universal dimensions and scope that symbolically enfold all of humanity into its death grip.

In a literal and superficial sense, the setting for the poem is this. A mother is on an overcrowded train being transported to Auschwitz or some

---

7   Alexander, *The Holocaust*, 91.
8   Shabbat-Nadir Hadas and Yigal Schwartz, "Dan Pagis," in *Lexicon Heksherim le-Sofrim Yisraelim* [The Heksherim Lexicon of Israeli Writers], ed. Stavi Zisi and Yigal Schwarz (Beer Sheva: Kinneret, Zmora Bitan, Dvir Publishing House and Heksherim Institute for Jewish and Israeli Literature and Culture, 2014), 709.
9   I am using the English translation to be found in David C. Jacobson, *Does David Still Play Before You? Israeli Poetry and the Bible* (Detroit, MI: Wayne State University, 1997), 151.

other death camp; the date must be sometime between 1942 and 1945. She has one son with her; the other, her older son, is missing. In all the confusion and cruel events of the war, this first child has become separated from her in one way or another—either he had been rounded up in a different *Aktion*, had run off to join the partisans, or simply disappeared. She wishes whoever finds the pencilled note left in the railway wagon to pass on a message, a message that is cut off, so that the letter she wrote is a mere fragment. However, that she is named Eve and has two sons, one called Abel, the first victim, and the other Cain, the first-born, positions the opus in a transhistorical posture.

She is called Eve (*Chava*) on the train because the circumstances have turned the literal reality into an allusion and a parable, so that her innocent child, Abel (*Hevel*), already dead in the first biblical account of a slaying by the hand of his older brother, is doomed like everyone else in the railway car, while Cain (*Kayin*) has fled, hiding from God's vengeance. Yet, like Abel, he, too, is a "son of Adam," generically and morally a human being. This may be what Eve wants to tell him, that, despite his killing of Abel in a fit of jealousy and rage, he is still her son and Adam's.

The starkness of the language is one of the central aspects of the poem's meaning. One is compelled to ask what is the difference between a sealed car or chest and this carload, transport, or wagon in the opening line. "The sealed railway wagon," as Eric Smith points out, is "one of the many symbols of the Holocaust" alluded to in the poem[10] and is, in fact, the closest thing to an explicit object, thus a synecdoche, a thing which is both factual and figurative, a part that stands for the whole. In fact, when one considers that in Hebrew, the word *Mishloach*, which in the poem has been translated as "carload," means a package or a consignment, it becomes abundantly evident that Eve is not only transmitting a message to her son through the scrawled note but that her condition and predicament are the message itself.

That being so, the nature of the writer of the pencilled lines, incomplete message, the lack of punctuation and capitalization—as well as the poet who creates this modern-day *midrash* on the story of Cain and Abel, and we who read and discuss this modern Israeli work of literature and Holocaust memorial—are all a metonym (a transformation of names, objects, and actions into a rhetorical figure of speech) for a sealed epistle, a secret message, a text that cries out for interpretation.

Lawrence Langer maintains that, "Poets like Pagis exalt the power of language to limn the silence: they write praise songs to the very words that

---

10 Eric Smith, "'Written in Pencil in the Sealed Boxcar': Voices from the Periphery," *Xenophile: A Journal of Comparative Literature* 2 (April 25, 2014): 16-18.

remind us of the calamity they deplore. Perhaps this is the paradox of all Holocaust art..."[11] Certainly, Pagis captures the silence of memory and frames it in the language of implication and allusion. Eve's incomplete note is a defiant gesture of bearing witness in the silence of death, and functions as a memorial to those whose voices were cut off and lives erased. As Ruth Whitman aptly puts it, in this poem "...we see the whole Jewish people, in fact all the sufferers and victims of the civilized world stifling the sealed railway car on its way to Auschwitz, the whole of mankind personified in the grieving mother Eve."[12] In another reading, Pagis is transmuted into Eve, who is "...confounded by the permeant division between victim and murdered in her own progeny, and unable even to convey her desperation."[13]

The tightness of the ancient Hebrew names makes word play, with etymological play on its consonantal roots and homonymic affiliations, essential to interpretation of the passage. It is not quite that things are the consequence of names but that names point toward prior motivations, present circumstances, and future relationships. Adam is the first man by chronological priority and epitomizes all human beings as a father to those who grow from his seed. Eve is the source and essence of organic life. Every human being is therefore a "son of Adam," child of the earth, created equally by God's virile spirituality, and a participant in the life force that is *Chava*, the eternal mother.

More broadly, each one of us—every reader—is a Cain since we were not part of the those shipped to their death in the carload, and the unburied victims—our brother's blood—are crying out to us. In a post-Holocaust era, this shriek must encompass the survivors in our midst, reaching out to the present generation and pleading to be heard, to be freed from this hermetic tomb. The absence of punctuation emphatically stresses the need for continuous testimony to the infinite pain, suffering, and terror inflicted. Likewise, Abel exemplifies the more than 1.5 million children who were murdered at the hands of the Nazis.

In Pagis's haunting brief poem, then, the mother on the sealed railway car is going inexorably toward her destruction in the Nazi death camps enclosed with son Abel beside her, while the older, other son, Cain, has been separated from those doomed to extinction. What is not explicitly stated in the poem is that Adam is not there on the train, already removed

---

11   Lawrence Langer, ed., *Art from the Ashes: A Holocaust Anthology* (New York: Oxford University Press, 1995), 585.
12   Ruth Whitman, "Motor Car, Bomb, God: Israeli Poetry in Translation" *The Massachusetts Review* 23, no 2 (Summer, 1982): 317.
13   Alexander, *The Holocaust*, 92.

and dead to the world. The message that Eve writes in pencil and that she wishes the missing son to know—the facts about her current position and the impending end of her existence—are the culmination and the inevitable consequence of the first fratricide, or perhaps that she and Abel are together in these last moments, or that she is thinking about Cain and Adam at this time.

In a sense, Cain is incarnate in the agents of evil and sin, embodying the Nazis carrying out their Final Solution to the Jewish Question. Tellingly, this would indicate that the Nazis are not alien beings, a different species of beast, but rather part of the original and only family of mankind, who—like Cain—were driven by envy, suspicion, and base human impulses to murder the eternal sufferer, victim, and scapegoat, Abel. Susan Gubar maintains that in addition to reimagining Jews and Germans as siblings condemned to destruction and to atonement, the poem also denounces God, whose "capricious withholding and bestowing of love trigger an ire that instigates violence and suffering."[14]

All life, in this sense, is ephemeral and, like the word Abel (*Hevel* in Hebrew), a *hevel*—"a nothingness"—or in Shakespearean terms, a passing shadow, a breath of wind that blows out the candle of history, a meaningless and empty dream. The word also means "nonsense" or "nonsensical," perhaps alluding to the pointlessness associated with the monstrosities perpetrated against the Jews or the desolate feeling of futility often linked to the task of articulating and rendering the indescribable grief and suffering into words. Moreover, we are struck that Eve still relates to Cain as a son, reminding the world that in concrete terms he is a human being, the son of Adam. Yet, on a different reading, one could argue that by underlining the kinship to Adam, the father, that Eve is distancing herself from her aberrant, wicked son.

The intended recipient of the incomplete, open-ended letter, with whatever it is that Eve wanted to tell Cain about her final condition, may be a fictionalized historical person, one of the Jews in the camps who cleans out the boxcars after the latest train load of victims have been delivered for annihilation who may know Cain. Or it may be an historian of the Shoah who finds the note while studying the rusting railway wagon for evidence of how its suffering Jews behaved on this journey to hell and publishes it as a witness to the mind of one woman on the transport. Or it may be the poet who finds the verses in his own imagination as a way of consolidating otherwise unspeakable truths about the meaning of such an enormity of

---

14   Susan Gubar, "The Long and the Short of Holocaust Verse," *New Literary History* 35, no. 3 (Summer 2004), 448.

evil. Or it may be that there never was such a poem and therefore there is no reader at all and our role as readers is an illusion, a painful mockery of a memory that cannot be expressed, a terrible frustration.

For Karl Plank, Eve's declaration that she is "here" is not simply a statement of fact about her whereabouts inside the sealed boxcar; it positions the reader as an oppositional presence who cannot be "here," underscoring the inevitable gulf that yawns between the now and then. Further, Plank maintains that the poem identifies those standing outside the sealed chamber with Cain either as the executioners or the bystanders, inviting the recipient of Eve's command, "Tell him that I" to perform an act that figuratively and literally unlocks the chamber confining Eve and:

> If the reader is to avoid remaining Cain, he or she must somehow move from outside to inside the boxcar. Eve's imperative demands more than simple contact with Cain: To "tell him" is to transform him so the weight of the heavy emptiness becomes his own, so he becomes present among the sufferers as their witness instead of their oppressor. So, Eve's isolation comes to an end.[15]

According to Plank, this opus confects a channel of communication and a mode of listening that enables readers to forswear the risk of being assigned the character of Cain, given their location outside the carload. In this context, one could observe that the reader is commanded to partake in the process of memorialization by not only forging a connection with the traumatic past but by completing and delivering Eve's truncated message to a contemporary audience and thereby bequeathing her with a voice that speaks and engages directly with those communities who have not known the horrors. In other words, we are enlisted in the mission of witnessing and are summoned to enact the ritual of *Zachor* so crucial to Holocaust discourse and commemoration.

Indeed, it is not clear whether the letter was written on a piece of paper or other material to be left for someone to find and deliver to her older son or whether the writing was inscribed on the wall of the sealed car. In either case, by writing in pencil, the message can easily be smudged and fade away, thus adding to its fleeting status, or as Gubar puts it, "…its soon-to-fade ephemeral erasability."[16]

---

15   Karl Plank, *Mother of the Wire Fence: Inside and Outside the Holocaust* (Louisville, KY: Westminster John Knox Press, 1994), 49–50.
16   Gubar, "The Long and the Short," 448.

"Chilling as it may be, though," writes Naomi Sokoloff, "the conclusion to '*Katub be 'ipparon*' leaves an indeterminate state of affairs and so there is room for hope."[17] Additionally, Wendy Zierler maintains that since the poem encompasses at once a mythical and universal message, Eve's message:

> ...functions both as a response to the specific historical situation of the Holocaust and a general response to the murderous history of the world. On a specific level, her scrawling exemplifies the desperate efforts of so many Jewish Holocaust victims to bear witness. The lack of closure to her message metonymically and mimetically symbolizes the abruptness of their deaths and their resultant inability to complete their testimony... On a more general level, her message operates like a broken record of universal memory.[18]

Unanswered questions abound about the lack of closure, the ellipsis, and the abrupt end of the poem in mid-sentence. Did Eve suffocate in the confined car that contained no breathing room? Was she violently interrupted by the guards dragging her out of the train? Was her voice muted when her mourning and lamentation about her fate and the realization that the divine covenant had been revoked render her speechless? Did she escape? Perhaps she could no longer articulate in words the inexpressible and extreme loss she felt about the annihilation of Eden and her son, and deliberately left the sentence unfinished? Or was she simply weakened and diminished by despair and the magnitude of the catastrophe?

The complex layering of meanings and allusions in the poem goes beyond the ambiguities, puns, and sound effects in the proper names of the characters mentioned in the text. The first word *kan* (here) that gives the words of the mother her immediate relationship to the place and the time of her situation also directs us toward the name of her missing older son, *Kayin* (Cain). This hints at and references the alternative contexts in which the words gain their significance: inside and outside the immediacy of the sealed boxcar within and subsequent to the Holocaust when, despite the fragmented nature of the address to her son, the modern reader who has survived and regards the entire poem as both full of the grief felt by those who were on their way to destruction and their lost voices that have been recreated through implication, as well as the calm place of reflection in which we read and think about what has vanished. Thus, Amir Eshel

---

17 Naomi Sokoloff, "Holocaust Transformations in Dan Pagis's *Gilgul*," *Hebrew Annual Review* 8 (1984): 219.

18 Wendy Zierler, "Footprints, Traces, Remnants: The Operations of Memory in Dan Pagis's 'Aqebot,'" *Judaism* 41, no. 4 (Fall 1992): 324–25.

comments, "The poem does not let the time of the events and the silenced language of those who no longer speak fade into oblivion. Moreover, the Hebrew original allows the last line of the poem to connect back to the first (*tagidu she-'ani: kan...*) and thus stresses the temporal unity of the events described and the reading process."[19]

Rabbi Arnold J. Yuter suggests that "For Pagis, the Holocaust denies the promise of life and humanity"[20]; thus, he sees no future for the Jewish people, whether in their newly founded State of Israel or in the cultural and religious revival of Judaism in the wake of the Nazi defeat. In the limited perspective of the woman playing the role of Eve in Pagis's poem, wherein nothing is left of her family, community, and Jewish fellow victims in the Shoah, there is indeed no hope left. Unlike her original namesake in Scriptures, Eve and her young son Abel are equally doomed to destruction, her older son Cain lost into some unknown and meaningless darkness of history, and her own message to him and whoever finds or comes to read her message scrawled in pencil is left incomplete—a failed act of communication. However, that implied fictional reality in the sealed boxcar in which her final letter is recorded is not the only setting for the poem. Therefore, both in itself the text may be interpreted as existing in a different kind of mimetic space and has within itself, thanks to the Hebrew names of the figures referred to, the grounds for a less pessimistic reading. When Naomi Sokoloff describes how in the poem the reader moves "from the here and now into the eternal present of myth, and the effect of the biblical allusion is to universalize, to project the issues of the Holocaust into a general dimension that aspires to be of meaning to all,"[21] she risks trivializing the Shoah by shifting it from its unique historical status virtually to a general "all" of crimes committed *subspecies æternitatis*.

The subtitle of Yuter's own book, *From Genocide to Rebirth*, from which an earlier quotation was drawn, indicates that in addition to the cruelty and evil of the Holocaust experienced by both the historical and the mythical Eve and Abel, there is a possible way from *Genocide to Rebirth*. Does that make the poem optimistic, a sentimentalizing reduction of the Holocaust and a term available for general usage? There is no resurrection in a theological sense, to be sure, but there is, in the reestablishment of Judaism, its religious and communal institutions in the diaspora and the re-creation

---

19 Amir Eshel, "Eternal Present: Poetic Figuration and Cultural Memory in the Poetry of Yehuda Amichai, Dan Pagis and Tuvia Rubner," *Jewish Social Studies* 7, no. 1 (2000): 138.
20 Arnold J. Yuter, *The Holocaust in Hebrew Literature, from Genocide to Rebirth* (Port Washington, NY: Associated Faculty Press, 1983), 52.
21 Sokoloff, "Holocaust Transformations," 217.

of a Jewish State in the ancient homeland of Israel. The very publication of Pagis's poem in modern Hebrew in Israel followed by its translation into various European languages with an emergent tradition of Holocaust Literature is an earnest expression of that hope, granting even more validity and promise to that of *Tikkun Olam*, the repairing of a broken world.

Nevertheless, our capacity to understand and then generate new meanings through a *midrash* of the pencil-scrawled words of Eve directed at her missing older child require that we meditate on and feel deeply her current sufferings and despair. Her writing on the wall is an apocalyptic injunction. This hopelessness and sorrow was the situation in which the female writer of the hand-scrawled poem was placed. The fiction of a mother travelling with her surviving younger son toward inescapable death quickly reveals itself as a *midrash* on the story of Cain and Abel in the early chapters of the Torah. For the narrative's account of the first murder, with Abel an evanescent hope in history—he dies before he can marry and bare offspring—and the surviving son Cain in perpetual exile and yet the tainted source of all future generations—is only the first stage of learning from the text. Dan Pagis, whose studies in university and subsequent career as a scholar focused on medieval Hebrew poetry—with its riddles, mystical games of word manipulation, and allusive connections to apocalyptic and messianic dreams—has throughout his career as a creative artist sought to give voice to the inarticulate cries of all those murdered in the Shoah and to open new spaces in modern literature for a continuing engagement with the ambiguities and ambivalences of what remains of fractured memories.

Like the rabbinic midrashists, Pagis too is not totally crushed into silence by the initial impact of the words and concepts of the historical event. Sidra Dekoven Ezrahi attempts to bring the meaningful processes of midrashic enhancement of the text to our attention but almost loses the powerful sense of human loss embodied in the troubled textures of the six-line poem: "A poetry of unfathomable depths poised at the borders of language, of enigmatic signals sent directly to the reader, has yielded to a sane set of surfaces that beckon the reader to eavesdrop."[22] The problem is that there may be no "sane" surfaces left in the world after the Holocaust, not even in Israel's collective memory of the trauma because that memory is itself fissured and beset with controversies, and certainly not in our contemporary world in which Holocaust denial and anti-Zionist propaganda continue to muddle all the issues of suffering and loss. A reader may furnish an alternative

---

22   Sidra DeKoven Ezrahi, *Booking Passage: Exile and Homecoming in the Modern Jewish Imagination* (Berkeley, CA: University of California Press, 2000), 176.

contextualization of the characters, actions, words, and allusions inherent in the base text, which will yield new interpretations.

In the mother's pencilled letter, the first new context is that of an ancient biblical legend of the original murder in the postlapsarian world when Cain is driven into a rage by the failure of his sacrificed first fruits to be acceptable to God, the consequence of which is the older son's expulsion from normal human society and his being marked as a bloody killer. Once that second context is established, the long tradition of parables, homilies, and anecdotal analogies comes into play.

Here, then, the separation of Cain becomes salient, with the notion of this other son being an embodiment of the cruel Nazi officials devising and carrying out the war against the Jewish people, their history, and their religion. Eve's incomplete plea to pass on some message to this other son is loaded with ironic and tragic significance, whether the distraught mother wishes to curse her lost son, assure him of her enduring love no matter what he is presently engaged in doing (even as one of "Hitler's willing executioners," to borrow from Daniel Goldhagen,[23] or a mere passive cog in the wheel of the banality of evil), or pleading with Cain to remember who he is, a son of Adam—that is, a human being—and to behave as one.

For Pagis, in his putatively pencilled note found in the box car or inscribed on its walls and left incomplete, the text, ostensibly written hastily in some Jewish language of the period (Yiddish, Romanian, Ukrainian, Polish) is probably a manifestation of the poet's mother tongue, German, which he refused to use in his creative writings until the very last years of his life. Yet he rendered the text as Hebrew, the modern version used in Israel, although incorporating the classical names and terms of ancient biblical Hebrew.

The Book of Job's explanation that all lies beyond human capacity to understand does not satisfy. More than ever, the scale of what the Nazis did could not correspond with a belief in either God or a rational universe; it "beggared the imagination" as well as the faculties of common sense and logic. Abel's voice continues to cry out from the blood-soaked earth, even though God heard it and called on Cain to confess to what he did. "Am I my brother's keeper?" he responded, and for that he was cast out into the wilderness. Meanwhile, in the mid-twentieth century, Eve, travelling with her younger son, still longs to speak to Cain to tell him whatever it was that she wished to say.

---

23   Daniel Jonah Goldhagen, *Hitler's Willing Executioners: Ordinary Germans and the Holocaust* (New York: Knopf, 1996).

Chapter 3

The Prophet of Wrath and Lamentation

Although he did not experience the systematic destruction of European Jewry directly, having escaped Poland in 1930 for Palestine, Uri Zvi Greenberg's personal catastrophe carved deep cicatrices in the young poet's soul. This led him to plunge into his autobiographical and psychological waters to sculpt characters and tales based on his own heart of darkness. Born in Bilkamin, Galicia, Greenberg (1896–1981) began his career at the age of 21, penning Hebrew and Yiddish poems. One of the founders of the Yiddish expressionist movement in Warsaw, the three-time winner of the prestigious Bialik Prize published his work in various journals. In 1923, after personally witnessing the explosion of anti-Semitism, he moved to Palestine. As a matter of fact, during a pogrom in Lemberg, Greenberg and his family were cruelly subjected to a mock execution by the Polish perpetrators, a savage act that traumatized the young man.[1]

The collection of poems *Rehovot ha-Nehar: Sefer ha-'Iliyot ve-ha-Koach*[2] (*Streets of the River: The Book of Dirges and Power*), published in 1951 and awarded the Bialik prize, was the poet's anguished response to the Holocaust and is arguably the most magnificent model of lamentations in the pantheon of Holocaust poetry. Indeed, Robert Alter sums up the critics' enthusiasm for the work by declaiming that, "The scale of the book, its originality, and what must be called the grandeur of its conception, clearly

---

1   Colin Shindler, *The Rise of the Israeli Right: From Odessa to Hebron* (New York: Cambridge University Press, 2015), 60.
2   Uri Zvi Greenberg, *Rehovot ha-Nehar: Sefer ha-'Iliyot ve-ha-Koach* (Jerusalem and Tel Aviv: Schoken, 1951).

still sets it apart as the most substantial poetic response in Hebrew, perhaps in any language, to the destruction of European Jewry."[3]

Doubtless one of the classics of Hebrew literature, "received by Israeli readers as an indispensable literary testimony to the impact of the Shoah…,"[4] the title is borrowed from a Sabbath prayer that rhapsodizes the rivers of faith flowing with wisdom, representing the stream of bloodshed and tears shed by the victims as well as the constant wanderings of the Jewish people that ultimately led to the Holy Land. Eisig Silberschlag acclaims *Streets of the River* as a "grand elegy" and enthuses that it is "the most abiding document of the Holocaust."[5] Similarly lauding the collection, Ezra Spicehandler argues that it is "one of the most moving dirges composed about the Nazi Holocaust."[6] Going even further, Avidov Lipsker avers that the book should be treated as a sacred artifact, demanding from its readers that they acknowledge and admit its religious form and compelling those who "reach its gates to stand with awe as if before a holy object."[7]

It is noteworthy that in Greenberg's literary universe, there exists an acute dichotomy—a duality that is the golden thread running through the 385 pages of the vengeful utterances. The cycle of poems by Israel's prophet of wrath oscillates between passages that are at times almost involuntary in mood, exploring the horrible calamity, to imaginative modes of rebirth shot through with visions of regeneration. Indeed, Greenberg's *ars poetica*, while showcasing a tortured human soul that throbs beneath a cracked surface, abrim with feelings of mourning, guilt, and powerlessness, simultaneously betrays a shard of hope. As such, the poet renarrativizes the Holocaust experience, presenting it through the prism of the ancient covenant that God had made with Abraham and that encases within its midst ultimate salvation.

---

3   Robert Alter, *Defenses of the Imagination: Jewish Writers and Modern Historical Crisis* (Philadelphia: Jewish Publication Society of America, 1976), 106.
4   Michael Weingrad, "An Unknown Yiddish Masterpiece that Anticipated the Holocaust," *Mosaic,* April 15, 2015, accessed August 8, 2018, https://mosaicmagazine.com/observation/2015/04/an-unknown-yiddish-masterpiece-that-anticipated-the-holocaust/.
5   Eisig Silberschlag, *From Renaissance to Renaissance II: Hebrew Literature in the Land of Israel 1870–1970* (New York: Ktav Publishing House, 1977), 115.
6   Ezra Spicehandler, "Greenberg, Uri Zevi," in *Encyclopedia Judaica*, vol. 8, 2nd ed., ed. Fred Skolnik (New York: Thomson Gale, 2007), 75.
7   Avidov Lipsker, *Shir 'Adom, Shir Kachol: Sheva Mason 'al Shirat Uri Tzvi Greenberg ve-Shetaim 'al Shirat 'Elza Lasker Shiler* [*Red Poem, Blue Poem: Seven Essays on Uri Zvi Greenberg and Two Essays on Else Lasker-Schuler*] (Ramat Gan: Bar Ilan University, 2010), 139.

Renewal and survival are based on the age-old doctrine that Jewish existence is immortal and cannot be brought to an end. Amid the scenes of massacres and mourning, one discovers a note of faith—that out of the ruins, post-Holocaust Jewry will triumphantly rise to once again establish sovereignty in the cherished homeland, restoring the Davidic destiny in fulfilment of manifest national destiny. In that spirit, Wolf-Monzon and Livnat explain that alongside Greenberg's exploration of the satanic viciousness of the gentile and his cruel degradation and abasement of the Jew, Greenberg probes the "spiritual strength and sources of inspiration through which he seeks to restore the entire spiritual world that was lost with the destruction of European Jewry."[8] This is in concert with the poet's desire to examine a newer and more broad metaphysical thematic quilt that includes the "sources of Jewish faith, the conception of God after the holocaust, the uniqueness of the Jewish people, and the yearning for the rise of the third kingdom of Israel."[9]

Also looming large is the overarching topos of Greenberg's personal loss on which the poet hangs a large part of his jeremiad. For the orphaned narrator, the destruction of his childhood paradise extends far beyond the individual scale to include an entire people who stand at the edge of an abyss. To return to Spicehandler, he maintains the following: "For Greenberg the Holocaust puts into question not only God's theodicy but appears as a horrible practical joke which God and history have played on the Jew."[10] Yet, unexpectedly, Greenberg resuscitates the idea of salvation for the broken people, embracing the God he seemed to rebuke: "Thus, out of the ashes of the crematoria, redemption will come, and out of despair—faith. The Holocaust and the vision of sovereignty are two sides of the same coin of history."[11] Roskies further adds that Greenberg "was not tormented by the loss of faith; the poet could rouse the people even in God's absence".[12] And although settlement in the Land of Israel augured a redemptive value for the people, "What could not be purged, mediated, redeemed or transmuted was the incalculable loss of life. The death of the millions was unassimilable; it admitted no analogies…That was the cumulative force of Greenberg's massive lament."[13]

---

8 Tamar Wolf-Monzon and Zohar Livnat, "The Poetic Codes of Rechovot ha-Nahar ('Streets of the River')," *Shofar* 23, no. 2 (Winter 2005): 20.
9 Ibid.
10 Spicehandler, "Greenberg, Uri Zevi," 75.
11 Ibid.
12 David G. Roskies, ed., *The Literature of Destruction: Jewish Responses to Catastrophe* (Philadelphia: Jewish Publication Society, 1988), 567.
13 Ibid.

In *Streets of the River*, the prophet-poet stirs the bleakest depths of his seared soul and unveils a magisterial, philosophical treatise that renders the Holocaust in an inventive, outstanding fashion. To borrow Alan Mintz's words, in the collection, the poet confronts the extermination of European Jewry through a "…description of the procession of Jewish victims; the loss of self-confidence and engulfment by feelings of guilt and impotence; and a return to messianic hope and the vision of the Kingdom of Israel."[14]

Greenberg, a scion of a Galician Hasidic family, was au courant with the traditional Jewish model of liturgy (*kinah*), based upon the Book of Lamentations, which narrates the fall of Jerusalem and the exile to Babylon, among other events. Still, Greenberg felt the need to partly jettison the fettering canonical shackles of the past in his desire to evoke the vast dehumanization and murder, as well as his personal grief. As a result, his work is a braiding of German expressionism and the ancient paradigms of Hebrew poetry, thus creating a whirlpool of rasping invectives, abrupt shifts in tone and tempo, and apocalyptic visions reminiscent of Jeremiah and the *Midrashim*.

It is also significant that as a soldier in the Austrian army in the years 1915 to 1917, Greenberg personally encountered the brutal pogroms that took place in Poland. These seismic events ruptured the core of Jewish society and created an aperture from which it never recovered. It is not too much to say that the waves of anti-Semitic attacks profoundly affected the young poet and left an indelible imprint upon his work that would become an exemplar of secular national sorrow. Certainly, as Uri Shavit notes, Greenberg's overarching conviction, shaped after the First World War, was that European Jewry faced total annihilation because of Christianity's "imminent, existential and eternal hatred… a result of the impending transfiguration of the unending hatred for the people of Israel and the coalescence of dark forces at a given historical moment."[15]

What's more, Greenberg's recurring frustration and anger were amplified by the fact that his warnings of an impending apocalypse were not given any credence by the sanguine populace, but rather were rejected as fanciful, adding to his rage. It followed that Greenberg would proclaim himself as the castigating oracle, the only one capable of recording and wrestling with this traumatic and terrible calamity. Indeed, Greenberg is regarded as

---

14   Alan Mintz, "Streets of the River," in *Hurban: Responses to Catastrophe in Hebrew Literature* (New York: Columbia University Press, 1984), 178–79.

15   Yaacov Shavit, "Eschatology and Politics: Between 'A Great Prophecy' and 'A Small Prophesy'—the Case of Uri Zvi Greenberg," in *Ha'matkonet Ve'Hadmut: Studies on the Poetry of Uri Zvi Greenberg*, ed. H. Weiss (Ramat Gan: Bar Ilan University, 2000), 330.

the "greatest innovator in the annals of the Zionist idea, and one who has read Jewish history wholly and correctly: hence he was able to warn of the approaching disaster..."[16]

The cycle of poems in *Streets of the River* is typically infused with an extreme, violent polemic against the pillaging gentiles, freighted by manifold exclamation marks, stirring metaphors, epic images, and free, lengthy verse. And while Greenberg promotes the poetic persona à la Walt Whitman, the emphasis in this moving dirge is often on the national myth and the collective memory of the Jewish disaster. Neta Stahl observes that in *Streets of the River*, Greenberg eschews urging violence and the spilling of blood of Israel's tormentors. Rather, he now

> ...re-identifies with the old Jewish stance, distancing himself from "the nations" and the aesthetics of blood. Instead, he now focuses exclusively on those whose blood was shed... It is not God who bears witness now, but the poem itself, emphasizing the poet's role as the voice of the victims. This time blood does not trigger a poetic call for revenge, but rather a cry, which the poet transforms into a poetic lament.[17]

Stahl further maintains that Greenberg's role has been transformed "from the one who calls for blood to be shed, to the one who voices the lament for those whose blood had been shed. This shift is an important theme in *Streets of the River*, many of whose poems are meta-poetic and deal with this very question of how to represent the great *Hurban* (destruction) of European Jewry."[18]

At heart, the poems lament both the gruesome fate that befell Greenberg's parents and sisters whom he could not save and the victims that perished in Auschwitz. Often is the case that Greenberg references quintessential Jewish symbols such as the family at the Sabbath table, with a nod to the early Hebrew poets, while at the same time accentuating his own voice as a metonymy for the whole people. Moreover, Greenberg frequently describes the unspeakable slaughter through the mourning of his own immediate family, affirming the individual voice while stressing the universality of the pain. In doing so, the reader is positioned and is imperceptibly co-opted into imaginatively identifying with the experience they were excluded from. It is thus not surprising that in the immediate aftermath of the Holocaust,

---

16 Shavit, "Uri Zvi Greenberg," 63.
17 Netta Stahl, "'Man's Red Soup'—Blood and the Art of Esau in the Poetry of Uri Zvi Greenberg," in *Jewish Blood: Reality and Metaphor in History, Religion and Culture*, ed. Mitchell B. Hart (New York: Routledge, 2009), 166–67.
18 Ibid.

given the paucity of Hebrew narratives responding to the ghastly terror, Greenberg's poetry was used by the Israeli state in Holocaust commemorations and gradually assumed center stage in the country's official and public stance toward the remembering of the Shoah.

Overall, the message hammered home to Israelis was that there existed a connection between those Jews who lost their lives in millennia of murderous sprees and those exterminated in the camps—both part of a holistic chain of catastrophes leading to the establishment of Israel. Actually, Greenberg unequivocally underlined the notion of rebirth of the Jewish state and the sacrifice of the victims in the poem *Keter Kinah le-Kol Beit Israel* (*A Crown of Lament for All of the House of Israel*): "They in the blaze of battle and their sons—because of them: they have a land and a sea."[19]

The tempestuous bard's oeuvre is marked by an explosive rhetorical force, seething with exhortations and powerful declamations against the tormentors of his people. The speaker's individual persona addressing the reader accentuates the subjective, potent voice, conflating the political with the personal. Not infrequently, the "I" is employed to dramatize the horrors endured by the European Jew and the nation, suffering destruction and clinging to their eternal longing for redemption. Skirting along the edge of egocentric obsessiveness and with an intense sense of thunderous fury, Greenberg assumes the role of a biblical prophet to bemoan the devastating terror of the Holocaust, willing to confront and denounce the God who, instead of sheltering his chosen people, had surrendered them to the murderous gentiles. In one scathing poem, *Le-'Elohim B-'Eiropa* (To God in Europe)[20] Greenberg beseeches God to wander through Europe and through its conquered lands, where the six million sheep of Israel are buried underneath the ground, covered in snow, victims of the Christians' "Winter of horror."[21] According to Aliza-Corb Bonfil, Greenberg embraces a transcendental outlook, recognizing that God is a passive being who observes the suffering of his people from afar and does not intervene.[22] She further argues that Greenberg believed that regeneration and salvation for

---

19 Uri Tzvi Greenberg, "Keter Kinah le-Kol Beit Yisrael" [A Crown of Lament for All of the House of Israel], in *Rehovot ha-Nehar: Luach be-Mavo' 'Alef 'ad Shir me-lo ha-Yareach* [*Streets of the River: First Introductory Tablet to Song not of the Moon*], vol. 5 (Jerusalem: Bialik Institute, 1992), 59.
20 Uri Tzvi Greenberg, "Le-'Elohim B-'Eiropa," in *Rehovot ha-Nehar: Luach be-Mavo' 'Alef 'ad Shir me-lo ha-Yareach*, vol. 6 (Jerusalem: Bialik Institute, 1992), 33–36.
21 Greenberg, "Le-'Elohim B-'Eiropa," 35.
22 Aliza-Corb Bonfil, *Where Words are Silence* (Tel Aviv: Hakibutz Hameuchad, 2011), 170–71.

the Jewish people will not spring from any divine action, but from human, prophetic activity based on the Abrahamic covenant.

Elsewhere, Greenberg confirms God's indifference, declaiming that the chosen people cannot rely on their creator for refuge, mercy, or protection. In complaining and raging about the silence of God, the poet contrasts Christianity with Judaism, betraying his anger at the lack of heavenly intercession: "The Jews did not have bells to ring God. Blessed is Christianity since it has bells in the heavens. And their voice passes over the plains now, in the springtime, flowing heavily over the wide landscapes of brightness and fragrance. He is mighty and the ruler of all: there is nothing to pass over, as He once passed over the roofs of the Jews...."[23]

In offering his assessment of the poet's central message about the divine, Roskies maintains that:

> Since God, the Shepherd-Seer, had retired to heaven, leaving no covenantal rainbow behind, the few surviving Jews would continue to whore after strange gods until the poets' rebuke, steeled by centuries of sorrow, would finally rip the clouds apart, making a flood of retribution descend. Meanwhile, the murdered Jews of Europe, whose treatment at the hands of the Gentiles defied all comparisons, would remain the ultimate reference point of torture and extermination.[24]

While the poet points an accusatory finger at the Nazis, he is intent on reminding us that the European genocide that engulfed his people is only but one link in a chain of mythic narratives that have divided Christian from Jew. To wit, Alter notes that, "Greenberg means not only to record the immediate pain of a people's bereavement, but to bring to bear on it a transhistorical perspective, which is to say, to fit the historical suffering of the Jews into a larger structure of myth."[25] In the same vein, Chaya Shacham avers that:

> Greenberg creates an analogy between the events of the Shoah in the 1940s in Europe and the decrees of the Crusades and the Spanish expulsion. In all of these, he sees a continuum of deliberate targeting of the Jews, and when searching for a reason for these episodes, he attributes it to the historical hatred of Christianity, a hatred whose manifestations recur in every

---

23 Greenberg, "Tachat Shen Macharashtam" [Under the Tooth of their Plough], in *Rehovot ha-Nehar*, vol. 6, 67–68.
24 David G. Roskies, *Against the Apocalypse: Responses to Catastrophe in Modern Jewish Culture* (Cambridge, MA: Harvard University Press, 1984), 273.
25 Alter, *Defenses of the Imagination*, 106.

generation…Greenberg establishes a broad context for what he deems an eternal enmity between Christianity and Judaism….[26]

The opening verse of *Streets of the River, Luach be-Mavo' 'Alef* (*First introductory tablet*) powerfully exemplifies this theme:

> It happened to us yesterday…but it is as if it happened generations ago / Encrusted in ancient parchments buried in concealed bundles within pottery jugs / We found this written in blood of black: / There was a flood of Jewish blood, unlike anything else, trembling, severed from the Exiles, / And even an angel who dipped his wings in the blood is murmuring—no remnant. / In Zion followed the events of Ararat.[27]

In deploying the liturgical frame to construct Holocaust memory, Greenberg is coming to grips with an emotional entanglement that is buried within his own attempt to cover up and suppress his personal catastrophe, namely, the loss of his family. In one dream sequence, the author visits his family home in Poland, now occupied by a gentile family that cooks pork in the family's pots and sips wine from Sabbath goblets. The narrator, shamed and distressed, admits that there is nothing he can do. Further, Greenberg depicts this tragedy in antiquated terms, as if it occurred in ancient times and etched in pottery jugs, since his cracked, weakened voice cannot contain the private anguish and therefore the pain must be stored in an archaeological museum of national torment.[28]

Ezra Spicehandler asserts that, for Greenberg, the Shoah is a calamity that will forever divide Christianity from Judaism: "The tragedy, in his view, is the logical culmination of the 2,000 year confrontation between the cross and the Star of David and the six million dead are an insuperable barrier which shall eternally separate Christian from Jew."[29] David Roskies concurs, adding: "Greenberg's Jewish response to catastrophe was one of unreconcilable oppositions: Because those who dreamed of redemption had all been destroyed, the nations were left to make their own choice between 'Sinai, The Tablets of the Laws, the God of Israel' and the pagan blood lust of Christianity."[30] In this ahistorical version, the modern catastrophe is

---

26 Chaya Shacham, *Bedek Bayit: 'Al Levatey Zehut, Ideologia ve-Cheshbon Nefesh ba-Sifrut ha-'Ivrit ha-Chadasha* [*Home-Searching: On Identity, Ideology and Introspection in Modern Hebrew Literature*] (Sde Boker: Machon ben Gurion, 2012) 169.
27 Greenberg, "Luach be-Mavo' 'Alef," in *Rehovot ha-Nehar*, vol. 5, 7.
28 Lipsker, *Shir 'Adom, Shir Kachol*, 144.
29 Spicehandler, "Greenberg, Uri Zevi," 75.
30 Roskies, *The Literature of Destruction*, 567.

situated within a broader story line in which the Jews, from time immemorial, have been subjected to persecution by the same archetypal enemy—Christianity and the Crusades: "Again, Germany, draws out its breasts and summons the people of the Cross to its thigh,"[31] we read in one poem.

Overhanging Greenberg's entire arc are religious themes—specifically, the Binding of Isaac—which is intimately related to his belief that it was the old-age libel of Jews as Christ killers that drove the "Gentiles" (a term he frequently uses to denote the murderers, which includes not only the Nazis but their collaborators the Poles and Ukrainians) in the fantastical quest to exterminate the Jews. Stahl again:

> …he depicts the Gentiles/Christians (and not only the Germans) as barbarian and blood-thirsty pagans, whose beastly desire has been directed toward the Jews throughout history and has now found its most triumphant fulfilment… Greenberg here accuses not only the murderers themselves, but also the silent bystanders…The effect is to blame the whole world… for the murder of the Jews, who were created in God's image with man's blood. The Gentiles, with their wild animal nature/blood and desire to consume human blood, have thus murdered humanity itself.[32]

Various poems center on the artist's close and extended family as he laments their death, though in the process of imagining their end, he braids the personal with the national, grieving over the fate of his destroyed people. He details the horror and the slaughter, accusing the gentile nation for their crimes and issuing a warning about the future that awaits them in a world absent of the Jews. Enrobed by Jobian desperation and protestation, Greenberg speaks of a time when a Jewish messiah will exact a heavy vengeance on those bloodthirsty nations, collaborators, and bystanders who perpetrated the unspeakable deeds against his brethren, bringing darkness into their world. This accords with Greenberg's religious and biblical schema in which the Jewish people are always granted redemption following a disaster. In fact, the poem *Shir ha-Ma'lach ha-Gadol* (*The Song of the Great March*) directly references the Jewish people's spiritual triumph over adversity, "…but our will to live, to return and rule as we once ruled, from field to sea, fortress and wall. We have not been defeated in battle, we have not been overtaken by the sword, have not been dominated by the teeth of despair and pain."[33]

---

31   Greenberg, "Luach be-Mavo' 'Alef," in *Rehovot ha-Nehar*, vol. 5, 7.
32   Stahl, "'Man's Red Soup,'" 168.
33   Greenberg, "Shir ha-Ma'lach ha-Gadol," in *Rehovot ha-Nehar*, vol. 6, 117.

The deeply veined sense of dejection by the lack of heavenly intercession and indifference is registered by the poet's employment of an assortment of metaphors and images drawn principally from nature, such as the sun, snow, flowers, rivers, and forests that function as an evil expanse that harbors and hides the bestial atrocities. Indeed, the primary locus of extermination in Greenberg is not to be found in the familiar death camps, but in pastoral areas. The idyllic beauty of nature—such as the sun, which is anthropomorphized as laughing while the crematoria burn the bodies of the victims—dramatically and chillingly contrasts with the indescribable human brutality unfolding in its midst.

This trope is finely illustrated in the poem, *Tachat Shen Macharashtam (Under the Tooth of their Plough)*,[34] in which the seemingly tranquil Polish countryside, fused with the Christian symbology of the church bells, serves as scene where the savage farmers carry out their slaughter, "Again, the snows have melted… and the murderers now are—farmers."[35] The ploughshares that usually emblemize the tools utilized to cultivate the land and which epitomize rural life morph into a device with a tooth that digs up the "fields of my graves." Later, when spring returns, the Jews have disappeared "Under the tooth of the plough of the Christians."[36] The author underlines the farmers' wilful cruelty when he writes that when the skeletons of the Jews are discovered in the furrow, "…the ploughman will not be saddened or shocked. He will smile…recognise it in the strike of his tool."[37] Concurrently, in another poem, the terms drawn from nature also serve to depict the slayers as wild animals and the whole land as a killing field: "We, the Jews, are now in this world, and all this killing land revolves in the heart."[38] For instance, Greenberg's fictively reconstructs the felling of his father in a snowy field, again, to underline the lack of God's protection and how pervasive is human injustice.

The theme of German barbarity looms large in *Lo Nidemenu le-Klavim bein ha-Goyim* (We Were not Likened to Dogs Among the Gentiles), a disturbing poem that shines a light on the wicked and their treatment of the Jews. The artist gasps at the love and care bestowed upon the dog by his gentile owners, who grieve at his passing as they would a family member, while denying the Jew any similar humane compassion afforded to the

---

34 Greenberg, "Tachat Shen Macharashtam," in *Rehovot ha-Nehar*, vol. 6, 67.
35 Ibid.
36 Ibid.
37 Ibid.
38 Greenberg, "Shir ha-Ma☒lach ha-Gadol," in *Rehovot ha-Nehar*, vol. 6, 117.

animal. According to Greenberg, the violation of the Jew is comparable to that meted out to an infected sheep:

> We were not led like sheep to the slaughter in the boxcars. / For like leprous sheep they led us to extinction. / Over all the beautiful landscapes of Europe… / The gentiles did not handle their sheep as they handle our bodies; / Before the slaughter they did not pull out the teeth of their sheep: / They did not strip the wool from their bodies as they did to us: / They did not push the sheep into the fire to make ash of the living / And to scatter the ashes over streams and sewers.[39]

In a volcanic outburst, the poem's coda contains the vehement warning that the desecration of Jewish life will forever be embedded in the annals of western civilization, destined to become the axis of reference for all human atrocities to come: "And there are no analogies to this, our disaster that came to us and their hands? There are no other analogies (all words are shades of shadow). Therein lies the horrifying phrase: No other analogies!"[40] Elsewhere, Greenberg references the murder of his father by a Nazi soldier on a snowy hill, the invasion of the Jewish home by gentiles who engrave a cross onto the walls, and a yearning to be buried with his parents for he cannot live without them. It is noteworthy that hand in hand with his escalating rage against the evildoers, Greenberg at times expresses disapproval and castigates the Jews, whom he believes were helpless and did not offer any resistance to their oppressors.

In the lacerating poem *Keter Kinah le-Chol Beit Yisrael* (*A Crown Lament for All of the House of Israel*),[41] Greenberg conjures up the haunting and disturbing image of the Jews marching toward their death, naked and barefoot, through the fields, toward the crematorium. Suddenly, he notices the faces of his parents, sisters, and their families. In one stanza, his nephew Shmuel pleads with his uncle, questioning his seeming lack of concern, and asking why he has abandoned him to the executioners and has journeyed to Jerusalem. Burning with guilt and shame, after lamenting the death of his sister, the poet wonders how, confronted with a world devoid of mercy and divine providence, he can pray and enlist the aid of heavens or how he can sit for a meal, embrace another, laugh out loud or express love while underneath him lie his family's silent blood and corpses.

---

39 Uri Zvi Greenberg, "Lo Nidemenu le-Klavim bein ha-Goyim" ("We Were Not Likened to Dogs Among the Gentiles"), in *Modern Hebrew Poetry: A Bilingual Anthology*, ed. Ruth Finer (Berkeley, CA: University of California Press, 1996), 124-126.
40 Ibid., 126.
41 Greenberg, "Keter Kinah le-Kol Beit Yisrael," in *Rehovot ha-Nehar*, vol. 5, 46.

Streets of the River is the only volume in which Greenberg subjects himself to such intense flagellation and serrating sorrow, most conspicuously when he recalls his own inadequacies and his desertion of his sister.[42] Certainly, Greenberg's absence from the death circle that enveloped his kin remains for the poet an injurious and macabre verity that he cannot come to grips with. In this connection, as Lipsker points out, the theme of theodicy that runs through Greenberg's series of poems, also brings into sharp focus and mirrors the poet's own sense of culpability and failings.[43]

Further, the poet points to his own inadequacy in finding the right pathways to reach God, asking how he is able to heartily praise the Lord in the absence of heavenly providence. Yet, burdened with sorrow and torment, Greenberg conjures up an uplifting tableau of revived nationalism that unfolds on Mount Sinai and in which the Jewish nation reclaims their ancient glory.

The intermingling of biblical motifs with the European genocide is further amplified in 'Elohim! Hitzaltani me-'Ur-'Ashkenaz ("Lord! You Saved Me from Ur-Germany As I Fled"[44]). Employing the legend in which God saves Abram from the fire (Ur) after being tried and sentenced to death, the poet equates the furnaces of the ancient Chaldees with the crematoria of Auschwitz. Further, the poet's survival (albeit with a scarred and riven psyche) and the shielding of Israel from Nazi attack is a redemptive affirmation of divine kindness and a sign that the holy covenant will be actualized with the return of the Jews to their homeland.

Above all, Greenberg's central message is that the supreme form of retribution will be victory over his people's enemies and the ascendency of Jewish pride in the land of their forefathers. In that context, one could argue that Greenberg is, in fact, propounding the Zionist principle of national revival, believing that the redemption and deliverance of his people to the Land of Israel is a direct result of the material forces of history, namely, the suffering endured by the Jews at the hands of the Nazis. At the same time, Greenberg does see the end of exile in terms of divine redemption, marshalling as proof of God's intercession the fact that Palestine was spared a Nazi invasion.

---

42 Lipsker, *Shir 'Adom, Shir Kachol*, 152.
43 Ibid., 154.
44 Uri Zvi Greenberg, "'Elohim! Hitzaltani me-'Ur-'Ashkenaz" ("Lord! You Saved Me from Ur-Germany As I Fled"), in *Modern Hebrew Poetry: A Bilingual Anthology*, ed. Ruth Finer (Berkeley, CA: University of California Press, 1996), 126–29.

Chapter 4

The Shoah as an Asylum

Yoram Kaniuk, who Nicole Kraus maintains was "Israel's greatest and least celebrated writers,"[1] was born on May 2, 1930 in Tel Aviv, Palestine, and died in 2013 in Israel. A theater and film critic, he began writing prose in the 1960s and became one of Israel's most prolific novelists. In more than forty years of prodigious output, his body of work has been translated into more than 20 languages. His complex and sensitive literary craftsmanship has been recognized with several prizes, including the Brenner Prize (1987), the Prix des Droits de l'Homme (France, 1997), the President's Prize (1998), the Bialik Prize (1999), the Prix Mediterranée Etranger (2000), the Kugel Prize for Lifetime Achievement (2008), and the Sapir Prize (2011). Though not a Holocaust survivor himself, Kaniuk lived close to victims most of his life in Israel, as well as meeting others when travelling abroad.

After fighting in the 1948 Israeli War of Independence, during which he was wounded, Kaniuk was sent to Mount Sinai Hospital in New York City to recuperate. He then stayed in America for more than a decade, where he encountered a group of Holocaust survivors who inspired him to contemplate a book about their sufferings. To some degree, his own wartime experiences and his conversations with Holocaust survivors in America provided the raw materials for his later writings. But *Adam Ben Kelev* (*Adam Resurrected*, 1968), which forms the heart of this chapter, is not a personal witness to or a historical reconstruction of real events. Rather, it is a profound reimagining by a literary mind that turns memories, delusions, and fabulous East European and Yiddish tales into what may be called a poetic epic of Jewish madness.

Kaniuk's most well-known post-Holocaust novel *Adam Resurrected*[2] (1968) is a journey into the surreal heart of darkness of a survivor. It is less

---

[1] Nicole Kraus, "Born Again," *The New Yorker*, June 12, 2013, accessed August 8, 2018, https://www.newyorker.com/books/page-turner/born-again.
[2] The version used for this chapter is a reprint from 2008 (Yoram Kaniuk, *Adam Resurrected* [London: Atlantic Books, 2008].)

about the historical events of the Shoah and more about the psychological effects and the life of those victims of Nazi oppression once they reached Israel. In 1982, Kaniuk again traversed the Holocaust terrain in his powerful novel *Ha-Yehudi ha-'Acharon*[3] (*The Last Jew*).

Kaniuk's notoriety as a "maverick" was exacerbated by the appearance of *Adam Resurrected*, which quickly became a *cause célèbre* in Israel. Commentators argued that for him to publish a book about Holocaust survivors was inappropriate and even immoral. What right, they asked, had he to speak on behalf of the victims of Hitler's brutal regime and what qualifications could be bring to the task? Did he have the sensitivity and the sense of honor to tackle such a topic? Yet, as Michael England argues, *Adam Resurrected* is a "maniacal masterpiece" and "one of the central works of Holocaust literature."[4]

Pertinent to readers everywhere is whether or not a purely literary genius can depict the psychological or emotional condition of Holocaust survivors in a legitimate way, especially when those survivors and their caregivers in a mental facility are fictionally represented as all mad, and perhaps as symbolic of all Israeli society, of Judaism, and of the whole modern Western world. In other words, does art trump history and historical responsibility to survivors of the most enormous crime ever committed?

The original Hebrew title of *Adam Resurrected* is literally *Adam the Son of a Dog* and, as we stated earlier, it very quickly generated controversy. For Anat Feinberg, who feted the novel as "undoubtedly one of the most original and powerful Hebrew novels about the Holocaust,"[5] the work marked a "…new thematic and stylistic direction in Kaniuk's prose" in which the author "confronts the ever-open scars of Holocaust survivors and their traumatized lives… in an expressionistic style, harsh, gruesome and provocative."[6] Likewise, in his reading, Edward Alexander enthused that *Adam Resurrected* is "imaginatively the richest, and linguistically the most inventive and energetic"[7] of Israeli literature he had encountered.

As noted, some readers were disturbed by the seemingly trivial comic tones of the novel, which they felt were disrespectful to the dead, the

---

3 Yoram Kaniuk. Ha-Yehudi ha-'Acharon. (Tel Aviv: Hakibutz Hameuchad and Sifriyat Hapoalim, 1982).
4 Michael Englard, "Adam Resurrected," *The Guardian*, December 13, 2008, accessed December 17, 2017, https://www.theguardian.com/books/2008/dec/14/fiction4.
5 Anat Feinberg, "Yoram Kaniuk," in *Encyclopeadia Judaica*, vol. 11, 2nd ed., ed. Fred Skolnik (New York: Thomson Gale, 2007), 764.
6 Ibid.
7 Edward Alexander, *The Resonance of Dust: Essays on Holocaust Literature and Jewish Fate* (Columbus, OH: Ohio State University Press, 1979), 106.

survivors, and the survivors' families. Others praised it as a story brimming with humanism, and found its political criticisms of Israel as a failed Jewish state refreshing. Still others found it an intensely moving revelation of the ways in which the Holocaust continued to reach deep into the Hebrew psyche to eviscerate its integrity and wisdom and yet was salvaged, transformed, and resurrected through the resources of Jewish wit and compassion. Kaniuk remarked on the role of comedy in confronting the Holocaust, noting that one can either tear one's hair out and scream, or "…laugh at the insanity of it all. The Jews have known it for many generations."[8]

Iris Milner contends that Kaniuk's novel reflected a shift and a retreat in Israeli literature away from "a judgemental position" that necessitated "a profound transformation in the self-perception of Israeli society."[9] Milner adds that *Adam Resurrected* and other literary works appearing in the 1970s and 1980s acknowledged that the survivors were "displaced persons so traumatized that no redemption, and particularly not a national redemption, was relevant to their tormented lives."[10] In a similar fashion, Yigal Schwartz argues that *Adam Resurrected* offered a counterpoint to those post-Shoah writers who strove to imbue the suffering of the survivors at the hands of the Nazis with meaning by utilizing the narrative model of the Passion or the Binding of Isaac. According to Schwartz, *Adam Resurrected* was the first to show that "the path in life represented by the road of torments and redemption was an empty shell, superfluous and phony."[11]

In addressing a question as to whether he lacked a personal perspective given that he did not experience the Holocaust directly, Kaniuk offered the following, which is worth quoting at length:

> I am an Israeli native. I was educated, like everybody else, to reject the diaspora. What changed my perception was my encounter with the Holocaust refugees shortly after the 1948 war. You must understand this was very traumatic for me; I participated in the heaviest battles and was wounded. But nothing was as shocking as my encounter with those refugees I had met shortly after they arrived in Israel from their transition camps and worse, in Europe. From that point on, the Holocaust became an obsession. It was very clear to me that I could have easily been one of them. When Israel accepted reparation money

---

8 Fuchs, *Encounters with Israeli Authors*, 78.
9 Iris Milner, "The 'Gray Zone' Revisited: The Concentrationary Universe in Ka. Tzetnik's Literary Testimony," *Jewish Social Studies* 14, no. 2 (Winter 2008): 123–24.
10 Ibid., 124.
11 Yigal Schwartz and Jeffrey M. Green, "Person, the Path, and the Melody: A Brief History of Identity in Israeli Literature," *Prooftexts* 20, no. 3 (Fall 2000): 327.

from Germany, I left for the United States in protest. If literature is something through which the absurd becomes legitimate, my writing legitimizes my attempt to convey the horror I did not experience physically.[12]

The literary text of the novel can be read as a very complex set of interwoven hallucinations, without there being more than a few passages in which the historical background in Europe or the current Israeli setting for the persons and events that appear in the novel can be credited with some degree of reality, or at least realism. Kaniuk approached the so-called "maniacal" subject of the book by creating a matrix of dream, hallucination, and Jewish jokes. This notion of the Jewish victim as clown and the genocidal actions of the Nazis as a grotesque carnival also stirred up contention about the novel.

Asked why *Adam Resurrected* received mixed reviews in Israel, while garnering consensual acclaim abroad, Kaniuk responded thus: "It seems to me that Israeli critics work exclusively within the context of Hebrew literature. When a book seems to defy the conventional norms or the established categories of literary generations or 'new waves' the critics are at a loss."[13] Adam Rovner agrees with Kaniuk that the novel enfolds within its midst transgressive threads:

> *Adam Resurrected* violates the entrenched paradigms of Shoah literature in general and Hebrew literature of the Shoah in specific, emphasising that absurdity, epitomised by clowning in the camps, is all that life offers to Adam and all men who are sons of Adam…The novel suggests that we are all trapped on a stage, inmates of a prison-world, compulsively performing a routine devoid of meaning without the direction of a revealed God…Kaniuk's novel presents a satiric and satyric subversion of the literary paradigm of redemptive suffering… Survivors find no transcendent purpose to their torments in *Adam Resurrected*; there is no theodicy, no "Passion," only the profane "passion play" of Adam the mocking saviour who leads a flock of psychiatric inmates into the desert. Instead of revelation, Adam only finds a heavenly father who is literally indistinguishable from a Nazi camp commandant.[14]

---

12 Esther Fuchs, "Native Israeli Literature and the Spectre of Jewish History" (Fuchs Interview with Yoram Kaniuk), *Hebrew Book Review* 8, no. 1-2 (Fall/Winter, 1982–83): 60–61.
13 Ibid., 60–61.
14 Adam Rovner, "Instituting the Holocaust: Comic Fiction and the Moral Career of the Survivor," *Jewish Culture and History* 5, no. 2 (2000): 11.

To be sure, there are historians who do not accept the premises of an artistic rendering of the Shoah in any other form than that of respectful seriousness, an extension of the Adorno admonition that there can be no poetry after the Holocaust[15] and that the aesthetic imagination—like normal language itself—died and only a brute, documentary representation or agonized personal witness are legitimate. Others argue that Jewish tradition has always been able to cope with the worst of tragedies by gaining a control over the memories of torment, the breaks in the continuity of community, family, and personal life through modes of wit, irony, and comedy. Still others argue that there is no way to write about the utterly irrational and insane horrors of the Holocaust except in terms of delusion and madness.

The novel is mainly set in 1961 Israel, with the principal character Adam Stein being returned to a special psychiatric asylum in the Negev Desert after a brief period of release spent in Tel-Aviv. Most of the action takes place in and around Mrs. Seizling's purpose-built asylum for the care and treatment of Holocaust survivors. But there are also flashbacks to earlier times. With occasional memories of other characters in the novel, the focus tends to be on Adam Stein's childhood home during the first decades of the twentieth century, his experiences in university in the 1920s, his life as a circus performer during the heady days of the Weimar Republic, and the first frightening and repressive years of the Nazi regime. After he is arrested, from the early 1940s onward, Adam goes through the great transformation from man to dog in the concentration camp, with scenes of how physical and moral changes in him are brought about during the inferno.

Following the war, from 1945 to 1958, Adam, exemplifying the next phase in the metamorphosis of Jewish life and character, attempts to integrate back into Germany and also into Switzerland. These attempts are only superficially successful. Moreover, they appear through the lens of the growing distortions of his feelings of guilt and encroaching insanity. When Adam goes to Israel to seek his daughter, he, like other survivors, goes through a new ordeal of assimilating and becoming a native Israeli, a Sabra, in a secular society, with settings in Tel Aviv and Jerusalem. Then, as the delusions become too painful for him to bear, he is placed in a mental hospital in Jaffa and eventually becomes confined in the newly opened Seizling Institute and its immediate surroundings in the Negev and the small neighboring towns. The time of the narration, when Adam writes to the reader outside of the hallucinatory experiences of the novel, is the early years of the 1960s.

---

15 Adorno, *Negative Dialectics*, 326.

As stated earlier, at the center of these experiences and narrative events is Adam Stein, the man with a charismatic effect on all patients at the asylum, who eagerly await his return because they believe that he has the power to give them a special, new life. The attending psychiatric doctors and nurses, however, are sceptical of Adam's so-called powers. Almost the entire plot is seen through Adam's eyes and is part of his memory. There are several strands of narration that look back into Adam's past and those of the other patients and staff at this mental hospital. Their memories, current delusions, and participation in various treatment exercises carried out individually and in groups at the asylum often overlap, and they at times seem to share each other's fantasies.

Despite occasional spells of sanity and self-control, Adam Stein is totally mad; therefore, his releases from the asylum are always brief. After an initial stint in a hospital for the emotionally disturbed in Jaffa, outside of Tel Aviv, he is sent to the newly opened hospital in the Negev. Some of the former patients and staff of the first home have moved to this facility, and everyone welcomes him, since he is charming and entertaining. He gives courses and helps other inmates who, like him, have been chosen because they are survivors of the Holocaust. They find different activities to keep their minds off the terrible memories that haunt them. He gets along well with the nurses and doctors, and they find him useful in their treatment of the patients under their care, as Adam enfolds them in his own hallucinatory games.

The book begins just before Adam's return to the hospital and ends with his later release and death. The plot centers on his relationships with the patients and staff of the hospital. There is, however, no continuous narrative; it is possible that everything that happens only happens in Adam's mind, including the conversations among others, the newspaper reports on the events in the hospital, or the night when the patients go into the desert to seek a vision of God. Perhaps, too, nothing at all occurs, not even the founding of the hospital. The only element that is historically real and true is the Holocaust.

From the moment Adam Stein awakens, while still in the pension in Jaffa where he has attempted to strangle his landlady, his take on the world is an ambiguous melding of factual reality, visions, memories, dreams, and poetic speculations: "Through his not quite meshed lashes he sees himself spread over the worn, faded wallpaper. Instead of stereotyped flowers, he sees his own image multiplied a thousand times."[16] It is in this kaleidoscopic

---

16 Kaniuk, *Adam Resurrected*, 2.

view of the world around him that Adam and the other patients in the hospitals he inhabits are connected. The world he creates around himself—or rather, the world he draws them all into inside his private phantasms—is, of course, no less a mad realm of the imagination than any of their own delusional states. But because this web of intersecting fantasies has them all cooperating in a single aberration, it provides them with human contact again.

Many of the people in the hospital had been part of the pseudo-scientific experiments Nazi doctors performed on twins. Therefore—like Adam—they, too, could survive only by dissociating from the reality in which they were tortured, and then interjecting into their own selves their lost sibling with whom they had seen and shared the feelings of intense pain. Other patients, having lost their own spouses, children, or parents in analogous ways, also created psychological alternates that they identified with, imagined as being present with them, and conjured up as having spiritual roles to play in their lives. On occasion, a patient or a staff member is annoyed both in the day-to-day life of the asylum and in the dream world in which they are manipulated by Adam.

Kaniuk deftly shows the reader how, at any one time, the patients may be interacting as suffering human beings trying to come to terms with their traumatic experiences during the Holocaust, reviving memories of the lives they led and the people they loved during normal times before the concentration camps transformed their whole world into a nightmare. He also shows them recalling how they came to Israel after World War II and their attempts to start new lives in the recently established Jewish State. The complicating factor in all this is that remembering for them also means resurrecting the families they lost and the tormenters who ruined their lives—in a sense, becoming the wives, children, siblings, prison guards, and insane doctors who experimented on them.

One of the ways in which these people, now assembled in the Negev hospital in 1961, survived these traumas was by dissociating themselves from their own bodies and normal minds, sometimes becoming their tormenters, sometimes becoming the animal they were treated as and made to live with, sometimes hallucinating a miraculous world where heavenly beings take care of them. These *projections* (analogous to a film projector casting its motion pictures onto a screen) of their own images of their multiple selves onto others and the *introjection* (absorption of mental images as a wide-angle camera focuses a diversity of scenes into a small, concentrated viewing space) of the others into themselves continue in the present time of the novel and include the other patients and staff with whom they interact.

Mrs. Edelson—the landlady of the pension where Adam has been staying since release from the mental home in the Negev—awakens Adam, who attempted to kill her the previous evening. He opens his eyes not only to the reality of being in Tel Aviv but also to the dreams and envisioned constructs of childhood, early life, and career as a famous clown in pre-Holocaust Germany. He simultaneously awakens to the unbearable horrors of the concentration camp where he was incarcerated and kept alive as a pet dog. The old-fashioned furniture of the pension reminds him of his former home with his wife and son, but it is difficult for him to focus on any one moment, as each image of memory slides into another, like whiffs of smoke from the crematoria where all he loved has been consumed. Adam knows, too, that he is soon to be taken back to the asylum.

He vaguely knows why he must leave, that is, that he is insane. Then, he is driven out of the city and into the desert. He arrives at "Mrs. Seizling's Institute for Rehabilitation and Therapy, Arad, Israel," a place which is at once brilliantly new and self-threateningly inhuman, an asylum to care for patients and a prison or concentration camp to protect them from the outside and the outside world from them. The hospital is described, and most of its inmates and staff members are introduced, as Adam passes down the hallways and is greeted by the people who have been eagerly awaiting his return. All patients, however, while mad in their own way—including, it appears, nurses and doctors—are nevertheless presented through Adam's eyes and seem to be extensions of his own confused consciousness. A special relationship between Adam and Nurse Jenny develops, but what it consists of remains to be explained. For, again, as with the chief psychiatrist Dr. Gross, the world described seems to have no objective integrity. Rather, it appears to be part dream, part delirium, and part shared fantasy, as well as a real place. Through the voice of the narrator, names change and it is never exactly clear whether the person speaking belongs to a single historical moment or one particular character even as the narrator seems to shift perspectives and evaluates this world in a state of uncontrollable metamorphosis.

Though it seems to be a historical section of the novel, this chapter begins with as much grotesquery and fantasy as any other, and develops into the same hysterical and hallucinatory experiences as the rest. Mrs. Rebecca Seizling—who at first gives the impression of being an eccentric American tourist from Cleveland, Ohio, arrives in Israel and attempts to see all the sites, then tries to meet high officials in the Israeli government in order to propose an expensive project she offers to fund. She is rebuffed as an impractical and bizarre personality, although the size of her offer prompts one official to probe her background and discover that she is actually the richest woman in America.

Seizling then meets by chance with the elder Schwester Schwester (*Schwester* being German for sister), the elder twin by three minutes, survivor of the Holocaust, especially of the terrible experiments performed on siblings by the Nazis. The two women, who hit it off immediately, concoct a plan to build an up-to-the-minute mental hospital for survivors of the Shoah. This plan would provide Mrs. Seizling with an honorable and fulfilling purpose in life and the Schwester sister with a way of doing God's work revealed spiritually to her as well as enabling her to create a proper place for her dead sister to live with and in her. The elder Schwester sets forth her ideas that inspire her, and which outline the inner structure of Kaniuk's novel:

> We were a nation…a nation that betrayed God. And we paid the highest price possible—we became smoke and ashes… Human beings who have been halved, quartered… During the day we may be complaining, yawning, making money, building houses, scrambling around as far as we can, but at night we are insomniacs in our spacious houses, our modern apartments, our magnificent cars, at night we dream nightmares and shriek for Satan has tattooed our forearms with blue numbers…All those numbers screaming and crying because they have no idea of the why or the wherefore or the how or the how long or the when or the whereto of it all…[17]

All of these Jews, suffering intensely from their memories and their guilt, "have turned this country [Israel] into the largest insane asylum on earth."[18] If she had a million dollars, continues the elder Schwester Schwester, she would gather all these survivors, take them into the Negev, where they would live in a protected and caring asylum, prepare to meet with God—and be cured. Mrs. Seizling accepts this vision as her own, and eventually convinces the Israeli government to allow her to bring it to fruition with her millions.

The lives, personalities, memories, and delusions of the patients, nurses, and doctors seem to have some basis in historical facts, but are ghost-like wisps of insanity, perhaps emanating from Adam's mind. Their entire existence is curtailed and fragmented by the crazed policies and practices of the National Socialist regime, the defensive measures generated in the minds of all who went through the ordeal, and the subsequent careers in which

---

17 Ibid., 51.
18 Ibid., 54.

survivors tried to live in a world that could not understand and often denied their realities. In his memory of how he was educated in German idealistic philosophy and aesthetics at the university, Adam offers a glimpse into the dangerous manipulation of ideas that led to the evils of the Holocaust and the shameful rationalizations still being made for it. If all this is a grotesque mixture of fact and fancy, reason and irrationality, credulity and insight, it is nevertheless something that approaches the truth. At the heart of the chapter, there is also the special romantic relationship between Adam and the nurse Jenny, their furtive sexual encounters, their deep discussions on the meaning of life, and their psychological influence on one another.

Adam's usefulness in the concentration camp consisted of providing entertainment in two ways: first, he was made to play music and reassure the crowds of Jews being prepared for entrance into the killing machines of the Holocaust, to calm down their fears, prevent panic, and make them walk directly into the supposed "shower rooms." In performing this duty, Adam recognizes his own wife and child being herded toward their annihilation, and instead of warning them of the impending danger—since there is nothing they or he could do to avoid this horrible death except cause a commotion that would elicit even more acts of cruelty—he smiles, keeps performing, and watches them disappear into the illusion that all is not as bad as they feared. Adam is also given a second role to play, as a clown. He is taken to live within the compound of the commandant as his personal clown, where he listens to the mad chatter of his master, crawls on the floor like the master's pet dog, and grovels and performs like an animal. He loses his freedom, his dignity, and his humanity.

From his first role of leading the victims to their inevitable deaths, Adam absorbs into his consciousness the knowledge that he has collaborated with the perpetrators of this enormous criminal act. Further, in regard to his own family, he realizes that by colluding in the deceit to prevent them from screaming and flailing in rage against their own murder, he has robbed them of that final assertion of rebellion, their only means of asserting their Judaism in prayer and their humanity by rejecting any cooperation with evil. From his second role as pet dog and performing creature, Adam seems to willingly give up his integrity as a person. Adam does more than humiliate himself by crawling around on all fours, eating from the same food bowl as the dog, and licking up to the monster of a Nazi. He becomes a dog, thus earning the moniker he is given in the title of the novel, *Adam Ben Kelev*, Adam the son of a dog (in the sense of being one of the race of canines).

As the war begins to wind down after the Battle of Stalingrad, with the German defeat a foregone and inescapable outcome, the master seeks to insinuate himself into Adam's good graces, hoping—as it seems to transpire in fact—to have the dog-man-clown lead him to safety.

The bribes seem to work; to save his own life and ensure some kind of survival in the post-war period, Adam lives on with the promised wealth and property he receives for services rendered. Some or all of the memory that Adam carries within when he departs from Europe and reestablishes himself in the Land of Israel may be a hallucination. In that version, the former concentration commandant Klein converts to Judaism, passes himself off as Dr. Weiss, and accepts a post as director of the mental hospital in the Negev where Adam is placed for treatment. To be sure, it is as likely to be a phenomenon whereby the victim identifies with the victimizer, so that Adam has multiple personalities or social *alternates*: he is himself continuous not only with the man he was before the Holocaust, that is, a clown, a husband, and a father, but also with what he became during the Holocaust, one of the perpetrators, a dog who has no moral responsibilities for or understanding of the crimes, and a broken and lost Jewish soul. Because the loss of his wife and children is too much to bear, he also transforms into them, giving them a life inside in his mind that defies all reason, and yet makes him even less the independent man he used to be.

When Adam Stein was taken aside from the Selection and given a chance to live by the commandant as his pet dog, he was humiliated and degraded as a human being. But this circus trick whereby man becomes a dog is part of a greater swindle. It is a hoax in which the very qualities that make a human being human are twisted and lost because the acceptance of the role as beast is not only consciously taken to ensure survival, it is unconsciously adopted in order to cope with the painful experiences felt and seen all around, the guilt in the face of such collusion with evil, the intensity of personal losses, and the inability to find any purpose in it all. In the Seizling Institute, Adam is not the only person to still slip in and out of the delusionary identity as a dog. Other members of his own family (brother, wife, child) return from the oblivion of death in such a metamorphosed shape or, which is virtually the same thing in such delusions, the Nazi officer who forced the role upon them, and from there to the patients, nurses, and doctors at the asylum who inhabit and constitute Adam's dream world; and historically, too, for "all the German mothers whose sons came back from the war wounded and blind"[19] and thus the whole world then and now.

---

19   Ibid., 82.

The reader cannot be sure whether a description of a man crawling around the floor and barking like a dog is, in fact, a historical scene verifiable by objective witnesses, an optical illusion set up for satirical purposes, a private delusion projected by Adam's mind or one of the other patients, or a shared hallucination generated by the structure of the Institute itself, as though it were a giant kaleidoscope meant to concentrate the collective pains and pious wishes of the inmates:

> "Come, monster, draw nigh," whispers Adam to the dog. Whereupon, as if by magic, the embodied sheet begins to approach the candies. Closer and closer it comes, until it snatches the candies with a paw that looks just like a hand (or perhaps a foot, eh, monster?), hoarding them, growling and retreating. "Eat!" The animal answers with a bark. "I was a dog once. Rex was once a dog. We all were dogs once."[20]

When Germany lost the war to the Allies in 1945, Commandant Klein was true to his word and arranged for Adam Stein, his pet dog, to survive the final days, with its forced marches, anarchy and hardship of defeat. In return, his Jewish slave helped the Nazi officer pass as a Jew, Dr. Weiss. Then, inheriting the estates of Baron Von Hamdung, his former enemy's ancestor, Adam supported his tormentor/protector in his new life as wealthy man about town, card shark, and investor of the money by bringing him regular payments of coin in condoms.

This was the life Adam led in Berlin and Switzerland until he travelled to Israel in 1958: a bizarre and unreal life, a life built on preposterous relationships and tenuous circumstances. Rather than return to the circus, the newly rich and emotionally unstable survivor became the subject of research into the paranormal conducted by American scientists. The reason for his journey to the Jewish state was that he had learned that his daughter Ruth, who he was sure had died in the camps, was alive in the new land. This report also sets off a train of memories about his family and what happened to them after his famous circus was declared *Jüdenrein* and everyone had disappeared into the machinery of the Holocaust—until they showed up one day when he was playing his violin to sooth the fears of the long lines of victims being led to the gas chambers and ovens. Until then, Adam repressed his memories and his longings. He had also chosen not to migrate to Israel right after the end of World War II because, for him, already hiding his broken soul within the carcass of cynicism and denial, "Palestine is nothing but a joke. Refugees, escapees, bits and pieces

---

20 Ibid., 108.

of humanity, chaff tossed in the wind, they cannot establish a homeland for themselves and not worthy, perhaps, of having one."[21]

Feeling that his supposedly miraculous and cynical life in Europe was collapsing around him like a pack of cards, he decided to make contact with his daughter through a letter but was answered by her husband, who recounts her story since her escape as a refugee and invites Adam to come to see his newly born grandson. Ruth's history is that of many other survivors, providing a context to measure the far more unusual experiences of Adam and the other patients he will meet at the Seizling Institute. However, though Stein feels an immediate sense of welcome in Israel, he cannot really begin a meaningful life there, and a crisis is triggered when some boys in the open-air market call him "soap," a reference to the supposed use the Nazis made of human fat rendered down from the bodies they destroyed. His good feelings wash away from him and he feels himself to have become a monster: "Adam Frankenstein Stein… a bar of soap in a nation of soap bars."[22] Only at this point does he go from Tel Aviv to Jerusalem to try to confront his daughter, but once there loses his courage. After a while, he places a notice in the newspaper mysteriously inviting Ruth to meet him. Instead of his daughter coming to see him, it is her friend, as Ruth died in 1958.

Another moral crisis, another mental collapse, another descent into confusion and madness—at each stage of which reality fragments, confounds itself with guilt-ridden memories, and fills out with hallucinations. By the time his son-in-law Joseph Graetz leads Adam out of the cemetery where they have gone to see Ruth's tombstone, Adam is back in the concentration camp and has become a dog again.

He is in a session with Dr. Gross at the Seizling Institute in the Negev, back in the earlier asylum in Jaffa, in the concentration camp in Germany, in Jerusalem, in Tel Aviv, everywhere and anywhere all at once, himself a man, a clown, a dog, a victim, and a victimizer. The child, nicknamed David, King of Israel, who crawls around the room and barks like a dog is another middle-aged survivor, is Adam then and now, and is a host of other beings in hallucinations, and whose own distorted minds actively join in this collective dream.

One could argue that Kaniuk seeks to show that individuals respond out of their own historical experiences, concocting strategies in their minds to survive both the Holocaust and the aftermath of irreparable pain and guilt at not being able to save their loved ones, as well as the indifference from

---

21   Ibid., 127.
22   Ibid., 133.

others who cannot or do not want to believe what happened during the Shoah. Like Adam, who sat down one day to burn all the papers that proved his memories to be true or that asserted alternative facts to his feelings and imaginings, they are all arsonists who, in one way or another, try to burn away the unbearable and unacceptable past. But if, as Adam lectures his fellow survivors, there is only way to escape all this madness and that is to laugh—which is the reason that he became a clown—and he teaches this lesson to the others, he then exemplifies the principle in himself and brings all their preexisting and newly learned performances together in the Seizling Institute.

Adam's special relationship with a dog-man is sometimes perceived as an avatar of Reuben Katz, *alias* "Handsome Rube," and otherwise the whole panoply of Adam Stein's inner demons, social alternates, and hallucinatory revenants of his family. In order to try to teach Handsome Rube to express himself in human language, Adam takes out an old typewriter and shows him how it works. He also produces *ad hoc* documents to make the dog-man that he is officially recognized and protected. However, as the canine performers are Adam as well as anyone else he imagines, the Olivetti typewriter serves as a means for the protagonist to communicate with his whole mental cast of players across all the normal boundaries of historical time and geopolitical space.

In this state of mind, Adam Stein remembers more about his past in the concentration camp and the process by which he was converted from a man into a dog, in the same way that the Nazi tormenter Klein becomes a friend, a Jew, and then Weiss the psychiatrist at the Seizling Institute. Of this process Adam explains to Dr. Weiss, "We are both lost, we have both perished. Our voices are the voices of ghosts. Jew to Jew, God to Son of God, man to father of man. You, my God, shall wait for me at the end of the road. I won't murder you. I can't, and it's a shame, a shame."[23]

Perhaps Kaniuk is contending that God may have died in Auschwitz and in all the other hundreds of camps and murderous acts of the Holocaust. However, to search for him, against all reason, to obey the Law when the Law has failed to protect all the victims, living and dead, that is Judaism too. If God is to live, it is when he is recognized in the tortured, suffering, and cremated Jewish body, in the voices of confused and humiliated people constituting a mythical voice crying in the wilderness, the howling of a dog, the chuckling of a clown, the ravings of a frightened old woman.

---

23   Ibid., 303.

Having returned from his Negev wanderings, Adam Stein meets with his fellow patients and the doctors to discuss the nighttime wanderings—recapitulating the Exodus, expressing his wandering mind—all of which have become a circus performance by clowns, trained dogs, and mind readers. Pain, humiliation, envy and pleasure coalesce into the phantasmagoria of madness:

> "The number engraved on your arm is God!" screamed Wolfowitz in a fury and at once broke into laughter. At the sound of these words everyone laughed, though the doctors despaired of figuring out their meaning. As always, no matter what was done to prevent it, a gap existed between the careful and partial intelligence of the doctors and capacity of these others to unite in a secret society rooted in unintelligible truths. Again the group laughed and the doctors cleared their throats and took notes in blue notebooks that had the seal of the Institute stamped on their covers.[24]

Thus, the engraved numbers, tattooed signs of being in a concentration camp, the mark of Cain, the circumciser's removal of the prepuce in remembrance of the covenant, all these signs run together.

One of the shortest chapters in the book takes its title from a used guillotine purchased by one of the patients, Abe Wolfowitz, "the Circumciser (who was never a circumciser)." Why he needed such a slicing device is supposedly explained in an involved story of Wolfowitz's life that winds its way back through the history of a medieval curtain from a synagogue in Poland, the Baal Shem Tov and his followers, the penning and influence of mystical books, and then an institute for the study of language, a discussion of modern Jewish art, and the speaker's own preference for paintings of large-breasted women. This rigmarole eventually picks up brief hints about Wolfowitz's daughter Naomi's death and his inability to rescue her: "I have bought a guillotine," he says, "that is able to cut plastic. If Naomi's head had been made of plastic, she would have been saved and God acquitted."[25] This absurdity alludes to swift and painless death, resurrection, rebirth, and a reversal of history's errors and revolutionary executions. As well, it plays on the ambiguity of the word *plastic*—in its original sense referring to the malleability or plasticity of a material. Then, once the brittle and hard manmade plastic was invented, the term came to mean something artificial and unnatural. Wolfowitz then continues, turning to one of the essential themes of the novel and its theoretical resolution to the unbearable pains of

---

24   Ibid., 326.
25   Ibid., 339.

memory, guilt, and hopelessness that the Holocaust inflicted on the Jewish survivors:

> I bought it so that I might be reminded of the atrocity which here, in this house, sometimes starts to disappear. Dr. Gross calls this the beginning of recovery—in other words, forgetting. It will stand here and I, whenever I want can lay down my own head and bring to a close the agony of dying, what I call fate's game of pretense.[26]

Wolfowitz's greatest fear is that he will forget what happened to his daughter and to millions of other children when their parents could not protect them from the Nazi scourge. If Dr. Gross, the head psychiatrist at the Institute, believes that he can begin to cure his patients by making them erase the memory of their losses from their troubled minds, he would himself be committing an "atrocity" or, as commentators on the Holocaust have indicated, continuing the Shoah, so that a an additional commandment has been suggested as the crux of rabbinic Judaism: never to forget, or else Hitler will have won and been vindicated.

The memories, embedded deeply into the bodies and psyches of their survivors, is all they have left of their lives and the core of their identities: there would be reason to believe in God if that were taken away from them. The newly purchased guillotine will therefore be a sign of an alternative to Gross's theoretical cure of madness, as a means of providing a different escape: self-inflicted decapitation that also punishes the father who failed to save his daughter's life. Yet all this is "pretense," an illusion or delusion, but one that is necessary to the historical dignity and moral integrity of the men and women who have survived.

Wolfowitz goes on, concluding his speech and the chapter, by drawing in a previous discussion of a sacred relic of the destroyed synagogues of Eastern and Central Europe, the beautiful woven curtain that stands between the inside of the Ark, where the Torah scrolls are stored, and the outside, where the rabbis, cantors, and congregants observe. This is a veil of mystery and a work of art covered in mystical images and signs, a thing that separates and a medium through which spirit and words may pass. His discourse, however, quickly devolves into the absurdities and madness of the novel's normative textures, with its mixtures of sacred and profane, and transcendent and mundane realities. Thus, the paradox of the indignities inflicted on the Jewish body, in life and in death, and its ability to survive, if only in agonizing memory: "The curtains may be found on the shoulders

---

26   Ibid., 339.

of angels and under the asses of loose women. The Schwester sister sees an angel of God in the stream of a Bedouin's piss. Thank God for giving me life so that I would be able to die!"[27]

Hidden almost in the heart of this bizarre chapter—bizarre because it covers many new locations and introduces several characters not seen previously or only tangentially discussed in earlier chapters—is the question of how to find a watermelon in the Seizling Institute. Something so ordinary as a watermelon, food a child wants and no one thought of providing or, if on the premises, is locked away in the kitchen where none of the patients, not even Adam Stein, is permitted to go according to a strict interpretation of the foundational rules of the Institute. A child's craving clashes with a legal restriction, becoming, as so often in the madness of this novel, the forbidden fruit, the withholding of which, according to Stein, is another atrocity committed by those who misunderstand the Shoah and its consequences. "It's nauseating," Stein exclaims. "If I could just get him a watermelon! Even one watermelon."[28] Cut off in mid-word, Adam runs about, trying to raise support against this misconstruing of Mrs. Seizling's intentions, and to again complain about injustices, now and in the past.

As he rushes about the Institute, Adam forgets what he was at first seeking, and each person he meets—or whom he conjures out of his imagination, for they are ultimately the same thing—leads him into his own and into their memories. Characters rise out of the lost past, speaking of injuries and frustrations caused by the Holocaust, whose presence in the present of his ramblings and in the place of a shared hallucination mark a map of suffering that continues ad infinitum. Whatever happened under Nazi rule, with all its unspeakable and unimaginable cruelties, continues to happen in the Institute when the nurses and doctors try to make the survivors forget their losses and guilt.

At one point, Stein seems to be penning a letter to his son-in-law Joseph from the pension of his old friend in Tel Aviv, near the Yarkon River, again let free on furlough from the Seizling Institute. His release from the mental home, however, is disastrous. By being deemed to be free of his hallucinations, he has become not a *tabula rasa*, a blank tablet upon which all new memories may be inscribed and a fresh personality formed, able to cope with the realities of modern Israel, but a *tabula mortua*, a dead surface where life, in all its painful complexities and humiliations and irresolvable griefs, has been scraped away, a kind of palimpsest, once impressed by

---

27 Ibid., 339.
28 Ibid., 349.

history's sufferings and torments but now unable to receive new impressions, a soulless and deathly mentality.

In Adam Stein's case, he complains that the moment he recovered he was lost, not himself, since he could no longer be a dog or anyone or anything else that he had been during his emotional illness. When he recalls, for instance, the nurse Jenny with whom he seemed to be having a romantic affair in the early chapters of the novel, rather than a nurse who sought to treat his many fantastic waking dreams, she is now described as "a marvellous lunatic" with whom he could no longer sleep,[29] confirming our presentiment from the beginning that everyone, everywhere and at all times, is an aspect of Adam's delusional mind. Precisely in recalling those former hallucinations and the human relationships they fostered in order to fill the gap between the previous normalcy of life before the Holocaust, and all attempts at accommodating reality since his arrival in Israel, the madness creeps in again. He is not sure, however, whether he is ready to accept them for what they are and embrace them in place of sanity, with all its loneliness and sterile activities.

In writing this letter, Stein reveals himself—his inner core of doubts and delusions—while holding himself together enough to keep up the performance of normalcy and sanity for the outside world so that he is not returned to the asylum in the desert. The novel ends with a simulation of logic that is an actual demonstration of Stein on the edge of insanity: "Joseph my dear, goodbye and good luck. Would that everything which has happened will never happen again, and that whatever will happen may, in fact, not happen, and may all dogs talk to one another."[30]

Our perspective on all this, more than seventy years after the Shoah, contains the swirl of mixed mimetic levels of reality. First, there are the different manners of imitating what people believe they have lived through as historical events and individual life-forming stages in their personal careers. Then, there is what their minds have done with those overwhelmingly painful recollections, constituted as fantasies to help them cope with such physical abuse, social humiliations, domestic and professional losses, necessary guilty actions, and wave after wave of psychological disorientation. Third, there are the denials of truth that leave gaping holes filled with substitute people and events, bizarre adaptations of the other's (the tormentor's, the absent loved one's, the mythical, legendary, and fancied savior's) appearance, self-history, and powerful mastery over the destroyed original self.

---

29   Ibid., 361.
30   Ibid., 370.

In another sense, the more than fifty years since Kaniuk wrote and published his novel is a historical period of Jewish and Israeli history in which the Holocaust could begin to be squarely observed and studied in ways that were too difficult to achieve beforehand. The Eichmann Trial in Jerusalem played an important part in this shift in mentality by doing to the Jewish sensibility what the Nuremberg Trials (1945–49), after the Allied defeat of the Nazis, never fully made possible. Thus, Kaniuk's novel can now be viewed in a wider perspective as part of a Jewish and Israeli debate on the meaning of the Holocaust, both in itself for those who died and survived the events and in its long-term influences on successive generations who did not experience it or know its survivors firsthand.

It should be evident by now that one of the principal themes in Kaniuk's novel is the psychological damage done to many of the individuals who managed to survive the Holocaust. This horrific event was not merely an enormous crime against the Jewish people—a systematic murdering of six million men, women, and children and the destruction of their culture and civilization in Europe—but also a deep rent in their history, separating centuries of persecution, exile, and isolation, during which tools were found from within the different communities, separated as they were from one another, to maintain religious, social, educational, and financial institutions, and to change their sensibilities to fit in with the surrounding societies, no matter how hostile they were. For no matter how harsh the treatment and extensive the boundaries of exclusion had been, no one had ever before attempted to eradicate the Jews as a biological entity. Jews had been hated and exploited, to be sure, but they had been also protected as a witness to Christian truths, used for economic purposes detrimental to their own welfare, and shifted from one part of the world to another. The Nazi program set out at the Wannsee Conference at the end of 1942 was to make Europe *Jüdenrein,* cleansed of all Jews.

In order to cope with personal, epistemological, and spiritual losses during this period of mass persecution and murder, many strategies of the human mind were set in motion, mechanisms familiar to those who study psychological trauma under conditions of infantile and adolescent crisis; social, political, and natural disasters; and proximity to persons whose previous suffering has not been resolved or controlled. Such strategies include the suppression of memory, the dissociation from pain and humiliation, and the formation of multiple personalities. For Jews—whether Ashkenazi, Sephardic, or secular—customary methods specific to Jewish tradition, such as integrating private memories into inherited religious myths and legends, adjustment of liturgical prayers, holiday texts, and collective writing of local and cultural Memory Books of Remembrance, proved inadequate. During and after the Shoah itself, not only were whole extended families obliterated and communities destroyed but individuals were separated from loved ones forever, and whole populations of relatives, friends, and colleagues disappeared without a trace. Many lost faith in the ability of Jewish authorities, institutions, and formalized memories to provide any comfort or material from which to reconstitute their normal existence.

As Kaniuk shows throughout *Adam Resurrected*, alienation of the self from its own identity became widespread as irrational substitutes came into being with only temporary force to assuage pains, losses, and guilt. Customs, language, and emotional patterns of behavior broke down into which, if at all, only shared fantasies could flow—often out as well as in—making any accommodation to an indifferent, misunderstanding, or even hostile world all but impossible. Another key theme in Kaniuk's novel is therefore the way in which Adam Steiner is able to bring together (in reality or in fantasy is never clear) the suffering souls of the survivors gathered into Mrs. Seizling's Institute and to bind their fantastic alternative lives—or, rather, hallucinated alternatives to real life—into a new dynamic fabric: a tapestry that winds and unwinds, like the shroud, made by Penelope, seemingly abandoned by Odysseus, for her father-in-law Laertes, constantly projecting images, stories, and relationships that substitute real memories and domestic continuity with lost loved ones. Insofar as they understand the process, the nurses and doctors see merit in this phenomenon of shared trance-like behavior, not because it is a cure, but because it a form of palliative care, a way of staving off complete collapse of the mind and heart. The patients can then live out their damaged and disrupted lives with some sense of personal meaning and social cohesion.

As in other novels of the twentieth century, *Adam Resurrected* focuses on an asylum as at once a microcosm of a sick world—as in Thomas Mann's *Magic Mountain* or Aleksandr Solzhenitsyn's *Cancer Ward*—but also as a meditation on the limits of the Jewish mentality. These kinds of novels take the asylum and hospital as the ultimate expression of a sick world, one in the decadence that preceded World War I or as the epitome of Communist oppression.

Kaniuk's *Adam Resurrected* combines the two representative types. On the one hand, there is the Seizling Institute, with the best of intentions insofar as it becomes a distorted image of Adam Stein's mind and mirrors Israel, Judaism, and the world as having been driven mad by the Holocaust. On the other hand, instead of satirizing mental health therapies or theories, the Institute modifies them positively in terms of a mild amelioration of suffering into a community of mutually supportive fantasies. It is not so much that physical and psychical illnesses are deeply involved with one another or that reason and emotion (subjectivity and imagination) need to be in balance. Rather, it is that the historical reality of the world at best juxtaposes varieties of good and evil, though the triumph of wickedness and violence seems to prevail most of the time. There are occasionally moments when the imagination functions to transform tragedy into comedy or into a series of comforting jokes.

Chapter 5

And He Survived "Planet Auschwitz"

One of the first memoirists to bear witness about the incomprehensible terrors of the Holocaust was Auschwitz survivor Yehiel Dinur, most well known under his pen name Ka-Tzetnik 135633. His accounts and chronicles, exploring in excruciating and stomach-churning detail the horrors and obscenity of concentration camp life, were for many Israeli teens the initial gateway into "Planet Auschwitz"—a term he coined and with which he is most associated—especially since the tales were able to generate and activate visceral identification with the characters. Rifkin neatly sums Dinur's early literary legacy:

> The Holocaust was relegated so far to the back of the national consciousness that by the 1950s virtually the only reference to it came in the form of books by Auschwitz survivor Yechiel Dinur. Dinur's works, generally described as mixtures of memoir and fiction, came out under the pen name Ka-Tzetnik 135633...But they often featured tales that were so sexually lurid and perverse that they might well be described as Holocaust-meets-Pulp Fiction, and many an adolescent Israeli male kept one or more of these books secreted in the back of his bedside drawer.[1]

When Dinur labelled Auschwitz "the other planet," he reminded the public that the bestial killing center could not and should not be considered as part of the normal world. To be sure, Dinur saw Auschwitz as a separate planetary body, set apart from earth, noting in his testimony at the Eichmann trial that the nameless individuals in Auschwitz lived and perished under a unique series of laws that were disconnected from any known landscape or region. Yet, in later years, in an attempt to, "restrain

---

1 Lawrence Rifkin, "Just whose Holocaust is it?," *The Jerusalem Post*, July 6, 2012, 31.

the mythical reinterpretation of the Holocaust," to borrow Warren Zev Harvey's phrasing, Dinur revised his initial characterization of the camp as a demonic, otherworldly terrain, now maintaining that it was "…run by human beings, not Satan, and was located here on earth."[2]

Time and again, Ka-Tzetnik's confronting novels, which were some of the first to tackle the descent into Planet Auschwitz, bear witness to the years he and his fellow captives endured, singularly focused on the sadism of the German guards.[3] Denuded of heroic deeds, the tales are peopled by ordinary inmates who, trying to retain their humanity, are rendered helpless by the depravity of their Nazi oppressors. Gripped mercilessly by his concentration-camp experience, Ka-Tzetnik admitted that his inability to unearth the right registers and words to document the past resulted in exhaustion and breakdown. For the most part, Ka-Tzetnik's semiautobiographical novels are graphically disturbing confessional pieces that allow the stunned reader an unmediated and acutely faithful glimpse into the eye of the storm, into the irrational nature of evil that shaped the author's life forever. Gideon Greif, who has vigorously fought to reclaim Ka-Tzetnik's rightful place in the pantheon of Holocaust authors, maintains that, "There is no one else apart from Ka-Tzetnik for the reader to encounter smell, feeling and atmosphere for what took place, to come a bit closer, a few steps, into the death camp of Auschwitz… without Ka-Tzetnik, an experiential understanding of Auschwitz is impossible. There is no substitute for him"[4] Further, Greif hails the author as the finest writer and recorder of Auschwitz life specifically because, in his view, he was a courageous trailblazer who did not turn his gaze from any aspect of the concentrationary landscape, no matter how ugly or controversial it was "He hid and buried nothing under the carpet."[5] Infused with a stylistic obsession for outlining the violence, perversion, and bestiality of the Nazi criminals writ large, and fuelled by an abrasive reverence for an exact transcription of the abominable, the painful episodes are informed by the attendant despair of daily life

---

[2] Warren Zev Harvey, "Israeli Responses During and Following the War," in *Wrestling with God: Jewish Theological Responses During and After the Holocaust*, ed. Steven T. Katz, Shlomo Biderman, and Gershon Greenberg (Oxford: Oxford University Press, 2007), 331.

[3] William D. Brierly, "Memory in the Work of Yehiel Dinur," in *Hebrew Literature in the Wake of the Holocaust*, ed. Leon Y. Yudkin (Rutherford, NJ: Fairleigh Dickinson University Press, 1993).

[4] Ofer Aderet, "Professor Gideon Greif Nilcham 'al Kvodo ha-'Avud shel Ka-Tzetnik" [Professor Gideon Greif is Fighting for the Lost Honor of Ka-Tzetnik], *Haaretz*, April 8, 2013.

[5] Ibid.

in the camps. Also echoed throughout the books are the raging insanity of evil and the fevered attempt to maintain, among the fire of the ovens, one's dimming humanity and compassion.[6] Remarkably, despite the geysers of cruelty and pain that he witnessed, the hard lesson that Ka-Tzetnik carried with him from Auschwitz was not hate or cynicism but rather a "positive and universal one concerning tolerance for the stranger in a strange land… a passionate belief in the need to work for mutual understanding between Jew and Arab in the shared homeland."[7]

Yet, notwithstanding the critical surfeit of representations available about the Shoah, the powerful literary forays of Ka-Tzetnik as a novelist and poet have been, until most recently, overlooked. Indeed, Omer Bartov has expressed dismay at the almost universal sidelining by critics of Ka-Tzetnik's corpus and the author's relative obscurity outside Israel, where his writing has garnered a consensual chorus of acclaim.[8] Leona Toker concurs with Bartov's assessment, noting that although Ka-Tzetnik's oeuvre has been translated into many languages and many of his books have been part of the curricula of the Israeli education system, "…academic criticism has not done well by him."[9]

In a similar vein, Anthony Rudolf, in his obituary of the author, rightly noted that Ka-Tzetnik's "populist shock-horror over-the-top tendencies have meant that not only has he not received the critical acclaim of a Levi or an Appelfeld, he is almost completely ignored by scholars and critics outside Israel… Ka-Tzetnik embarrasses the experts."[10] This is despite the fact that in Israeli culture Ka-Tzetnik has certainly attained the status of an almost official "scribe of the Holocaust and its terrors, in particular a spokesperson for the most horrific of Holocaust experiences—the one endured by inmates of the death camps, which at its forefront stands Auschwitz."[11]

Yehiel Dinur was born Yehiel Fajner in Sosnowiec, Poland on May 16, 1909. His parents were Hasidic Jews, and he was one of three children. He studied at the renowned Talmudic Yeshiva in Lublin and later enrolled at

---

6   Avraham Hagorni-Green, *Be-Chavlei Shalom: Masot 'al ha-Shalom ve-ha-Shalem* [*In the Binds of Peace: Essays about Peace and Completeness*] (Jerusalem: Reches, 1994), 145.
7   Anthony Rudolf, "Obituary: Ka-Tzetnik 135633," *The Independent* (London), July 27, 2001.
8   Omer Bartov, *Mirrors of Destruction: War, Genocide, and Modern Identity* (New York: Oxford University Press, 2000), 189.
9   Leona Toker, "Truth and Testimony," *Haaretz*, March 26, 2003.
10 Rudolf, "Obituary: Ka-Tzetnik 135633."
11 Dan Miron, *Hasifriya ha-'Ivrit: Proza Me'urevet: 1980-2005* [*The Hebrew Library: Mixed Prose: 1980-2005*] (Tel Aviv: Miskal/Yediot Achronot Books and Chemed Books, 2005), 148.

Warsaw University. A gifted violinist, he began writing music and poetry in Yiddish at an early age, becoming well known within the Jewish community. His first collection, *Tsveiuntsvantsig: Lider* [*Twenty-Two Poems*], was published in Warsaw in 1931. He was captured by the Gestapo in 1943 and transferred to Auschwitz, where he spent the next two years until rescued by Soviet troops from a death march in February 1945. As he recalls in his last novel, *Shivitti A Vision*, he was so emaciated, resembling a "skeleton who had been rendered speechless,"[12] that the physicians caring for him saw very little prospect for survival.

His sister was earlier raped and murdered by the Nazis; with his entire family and wife murdered by Nazis as well. He wandered throughout Europe following his liberation. Fortunately, he was taken by members of the Jewish Brigade, fighting alongside the allies, to a hospital in a British army camp in Terra-Viso, Italy. Once he recovered, and after completing his first novel over a two-and-a-half-week period, he clandestinely entered Palestine dressed up as a British policeman. In 1947, he married Nina Asherman, who became his trusted translator. They had two children, Daniella, whom he named after his twin sister, and Lior. Dinur kept writing until his last days, enclosed in his basement and often disappeared for months while penning his masterpieces. The proceeds from his books were streamed to a special fund that financed the printing of additional copies of his works, freely distributed to schools and educational institutions.[13] He died of cancer on July 17, 2001, aged 92, and weighing only 30 kilos. According to his son, Dinur asked that his death not be announced to the public and was buried in secret. He left a list of people who were to be told.[14]

Ka-Tzetnik's novels can be accurately described as profound fictionalized chronicles of hell, stories related by a man who was able to transmit the shattering truth without once lessening its true dimensions: "The books leave the reader reeling. Ka-Tzetnik's obsessional and stylised descriptions of cruelty recollected in emotion have the ring of truth not only because he was there, but because he shapes his material through a mythic and poetic imagination. His sometimes frenzied prose, bypassing intellectual

---

12   Ka-Tzetnik, *Shivitti: A Vision*, trans. Eliyah Nike de Nur and Lisa Herman (San Francisco, CA: Harper & Row 1987), 16.
13   Kliger, "Ha-'Ish mi-Kochav Ha-'Efer Aushvitz."
14   Segev, Tom. "Met ha-Sofer Yehiel Dinur, aval Ka-Tzetnik Yichye la-Netzach," ["The Author Yehiel Dinur is Dead, but Ka-Tzetnik will Live Forever"], *Haaretz*, July 18, 2001.

rationalisation, is often mesmerising."[15] Publishing under the pen name Ka-Tzetnik 135633, Dinur took the number from the tattoo burned by a Kapo soldier into his arm and the moniker from the German abbreviation KZ (Konzentrationslager) for a concentration camp inmate, stating, "I must carry this name as long as the world will not awaken after the crucifying of the nation to erase this evil, as humanity has risen after the crucifixion of one man."[16] In essence, the alias functioned as a representation of all survivors, with Dinur serving as a Shoah everyman, but also pointed to the reality that the killing centre of Auschwitz robbed him of his true name and identity. Dinur also observed, "It does not matter that I, Yehiel Dinur, pass away. The most significant fact is that Ka-Tzetnik will stay alive."[17] Moreover, after handing over the manuscript for *Salamandra* (which he composed in two weeks) to a Jewish soldier by his bedside, the soldier asked whose name should be noted as the author. To which Dinur responded, "The name of the author?! Those who went to the crematorium wrote this book. Go on, you write their name: K. Tzetnik."[18] Consequently, the soldier wrote down the name in his own handwriting as instructed.

To be sure, this pseudonym further reinforced the anonymity and seclusion the author chose to embrace for many years until his death, while at the same time ironically pointing up the obliteration of identity and individuality the Nazis sought to achieve.[19] It is worthy of note that Dinur wrote his first five books cloistered in an isolated cabin away from family and friends.[20] Besides the pseudonym, the fact that the author adopted the name "Dinur"—which means "of fire" in Aramaic and recalls the river of fire mentioned in the Book of Daniel—after settling in Palestine clearly attests to the motif of transformation through the inferno that constituted a central pillar of his corpus.

In 1961, Dinur, who had actually met Eichmann, was summoned, along with hundreds of other survivors, by state prosecutor Gideon Hausner, and

---

15   Rudolf, "Obituary: Ka-Tzetnik 135633." See also: Tom Segev, "The code of Ka. Tzetnik," *Koteret Rashit*, May 27, 1987; Yehiel Szeintuch, "Discerning key terms in the Writings of K. Zetnik," *Hulyot: Studies in Yiddish Literature and Its Links with Hebrew Literature* 5 (1999): 275–90.
16   Nizkor Project, "The Trial of Adolf Eichmann, Session 68," accessed December 24, 2017, http://www.nizkor.org/hweb/people/e/eichmann-adolf/transcripts/Sessions/Session-068-01.html
17   Shmuel Shnitzer, "The Eichmann Trial in Jerusalem," *Maariv*, June 8, 1961.
18   Ka-Tzetnik, *Shivitti: A Vision*, 15–16.
19   Jeremy D. Popkin, "Katzetnik 135633: The Survivor as Pseudonym," *New Literary History* 33, no. 2 (2002): 343–45.
20   Ka-Tzetnik, *Haimut* [Fatherland] (Tel Aviv: Hakibutz Hameuchad, 1987).

was in fact the first witness at the Eichmann Trial to give evidence about Auschwitz. It was not surprising that Dinur's submergence within the reality of the Holocaust was so intense, so unforgettable, that after seeing the face of the architect of the final solution in the glass booth, and testifying about his ordeals, that he fainted on the stand, overwhelmed by the blackening, nightmarish images of what he lived through. Unable to continue, he had to be carried out and later required a substantial period of hospitalization. Dinur later offered his own explanation for passing out in the witness box:

> At the moment, five minutes before the opening of the trial sessions, when Attorney General Hausner informed me that the judges would not agree to my appearing before them under my own pen name—I immediately felt like the man from outer space, who is torn from the pull of gravity, but has not yet arrived at another planet.[21]

Hirsch and Spitzer observe that this iconic moment of Dinur collapsing onto the courtroom floor in sobs became "a paradigm for the aporia of Holocaust testimony—the necessity and the impossibility of bearing witness to the 'Planet Auschwitz.'"[22] It is noteworthy, that nearly seventy percent of Israeli students, polled in 1962, remarked that it was Dinur who left the most impactful impression on them.[23] Tormented, it is small wonder that Dinur sought LSD therapy in order to exorcise the devilish spirits haunting the dungeon of his soul, administered in Leiden by Dutch psychiatrist Professor Bastiaans, who coined the term "Concentration Camp Syndrome."[24] According to the author, the four sessions were pivotal in relieving him of the persistent nightmares invading his sleep and in furnishing him with a key to open the door to Auschwitz.

In 2011, in a Plenary Meeting to mark 50 years since the Eichmann Trial, Israeli Prime Minister Benyamin Netanyahu remarked that still today he remembers how Dinur's testimony moved him and his classmates.[25] This is how Dinur described Auschwitz on the witness stand:

---

21   Hanna Yablonka, *The State of Israel vs. Adolf Eichmann* (New York: Schocken Books, 2004), 110.
22   Marianne Hirsch and Leo Spitzer, "The War in the Archive: Holocaust Studies/Memory Studies," *Memory Studies* 2, no. 2 (May 2009): 154.
23   Yablonka, *The State of Israel vs. Adolf Eichmann*, 176.
24   Ka-Tzetnik, *Shivitti: A Vision*, 16.
25   "PM Netanyahu's Speech at Plenary Meeting Marking 50 Years since the Eichmann Trial," *Prime Minister's Office*, December 13, 2011.

The time there is not a concept as it is here in our planet. Every fraction of a second passed there was at a different rate of time. And the inhabitants of that planet had no names. They had no parents, and they had no children. They were not clothed as we are clothed here. They were not born there and they did not conceive there. They breathed and lived according to different laws of nature. They did not live according to the laws of this world of ours, and they did not die…[26]

The strong emphasis on authenticity and naturalism is evinced and underlined by Dinur's own commentary on his role. When asked by Gideon Hausner "What was the reason that you hid your identity beyond the pseudonym K. Zetnik, Mr Dinur?,"[27] he replied: "It was not a pen name. I do not regard myself as a writer and a composer of literary material. This is a chronicle of the planet of Auschwitz."[28]

In essence, the thematic quilt of Ka-Tzetnik's sextet of novels titled *Salamandra: A Chronicle of a Jewish Family in the Twentieth Century* shimmers with a rasping objectivity that primarily dwells on the complete brutality and physical torture perpetrated upon the prisoners, the sexual exploitation, and the total dehumanization that was carved into the charred soul of the Jews. Accordingly, in *Salamandra* (*Sunrise over Hell*, 1946), *Beit Habubot* (*House of Dolls*, 1953) *Ha-Shaon Asher Me`al Ha-Rosh* (*Star Eternal*, 1960), and *Qaru Lo Piepel* (*Atrocity*, 1961), among others, the absurd and insane universe of the Shoah is spotlighted through the figure of Harry Preselshnik. Harry is the author's alter ego, witnessing and reporting on the ugliness and misery embodied in the surreal, and at times supernatural, reality of Auschwitz. Concomitantly, the prose is often deliriously frenzied, slipping into over-the-top, stylized kitsch and sadism.[29]

Unable to exorcise the demons of the past, the former inmate, numbed and tormented by post-traumatic stress disorder, was so haunted and besieged by the burden of memory that he considered all of his prewar output and life as nonexistent. Following his breakdown on the stand, the author refused all requests for interviews and rarely left his house. As a matter of fact, he retrieved an early book of his poetry that was published in

---

26 Testimony of Yehiel Dinur, June 7, 1961, Session no. 68. State of Israel, Ministry of Justice, *The Trial of Adolf Eichmann: Record of the Proceedings in the District Court of Jerusalem*, vol. III (Jerusalem: The Trust for the Publication of the Proceedings of the Eichmann Trial in Co-operation with the Israel State Archives and Yad-Vashem—The Holocaust Martyrs' and Heroes' Remembrance Authority, 1993): 1237.
27 Nizkor Project, "Trial of Adolf Eichmann."
28 Ibid.
29 Bartov, *Mirrors of Destruction*, 188.

Warsaw in 1931 from the Library of Congress, the New York Public Library, and the National Library in Givat Ram, Jerusalem. After burning the volume of poems from the National Library, he mailed the charred pages back to Shlomo Goldenberg, head of the library, along with a letter that urged him to set alight the torn pages, in the same way that "everything that was dear to me and my world was incinerated in the crematorium of Auschwitz."[30]

It has been noted that while in the nascent days of Israeli statehood the author's books were treated as pornography by its teenage readers who were titillated by the remarkably explicit portrayals of sexual abuse, his novels are now studied in Israeli high schools and by Israeli Defense Force soldiers.[31] Indeed, Ka-Tzetnik's writing served as an inspiration for Israeli soldiers. In an article about the Ammunition Hill battle of 1967, David Strassler relates the following: "The lesson of the Holocaust was also in the minds of the soldiers who fought for Jerusalem. Ofer Feniger, in a letter to his girlfriend, explained that after reading Katzetnik's book about his experiences in the Holocaust he decided to train as hard as he could, determined to be strong so as to help make sure that such a thing never happens again.'"[32]

It is worth emphasizing that the inclusion of Ka-Tzetnik's books in the educational syllabus flowed from the writer's particular wish that his royalties be directed to funding the teaching of the Holocaust, reflecting his deep concern that memory of the event be preserved. Incredulously, despite the hobbling, unyielding evil he saw, Ka-Tzetnik's vision of life was not entirely that of a broken man. Rather, in his later novels, such as *Phoenix over the Galilee* (1966), he conveyed the message of universal peace and encouraged common dialogue and understanding between warring Jews and Arabs.

Compelled to record the unspeakable brutalities of his tormentors and fearing that he may not live long, he feverishly wrote *Salamandra* (published in English as *Sunrise over Hell*)[33] over two and a half weeks in 1945 ensconced in a small room while recovering in a hospital in Italy.[34] Close to the bone and swathed in scenes of devastating violence, the work is painful to read. Yet, in rendering the seemingly unreal, it is a blow to the solar plexus of indifference, for it leads one to ponder the palpable, unforgettable sorrow of the victims and prevents a turning away from the distressing and

---

30 Miron, *Hasifriya ha-'Ivrit*, 148.
31 Bartov, *Mirrors of Destruction*, 189.
32 David Strassler, "The Heroes of Ammunition Hill," *The Jerusalem Post*, May 12, 1991.
33 Ka-Tzetnik 135633, *Sunrise Over Hell* (London: W. H. Allen, 1977).
34 Tom Segev, *The Seventh Million: The Israelis and The Holocaust* (New York: Hill and Wang, 1993), 4.

confronting material. Commenting on the novel's lingering effect, Gershon Shoffman, one of Israel's finest wordsmiths, opined: "The book overpowers all others not only in its insights and vision, but also in the naked facts… the author forces on you the feeling of death with a mighty hand, so after reading you feel as if you were also there, really there, and now you are one of the miraculous survivors."[35]

At the outset, it is important to explain the meaning of the original title, as it underpins the thematic matrix upon which most of the author's concerns can be mapped out. According to Hebrew lore, the salamander is a phantasmagorical animal that emerges from a fire that was burning in one place for seven years.[36] In essence, it denotes a being that has been born of fire and out of destruction, whose threads to the past have been bluntly severed, and whose entire being has been crafted out of the flames. During therapy, Ka-Tzetnik revealed to his doctor that on the way to the crematoria he hid in a barrel of coal, and that it was out of that barrel that he was born "as a child coming out of the womb of his mother, from the darkness to the light of the world."[37]

More broadly, it is this central trope that frames the dramatic backbone of the author's sextet of novels. Like the salamander, some of the heroes who populate Ka-Tzetnik's literary landscape have survived the total mayhem of camp life but have come through spiritually and physically demolished, recreated from the maelstrom of anarchy into another person. On another level, it has been suggested that since the cycle of six novels is entitled *Salamander*, the ur-message knotted throughout is that without those individual salamanders—those brave souls who preserved and endured the mind-numbing assault—the truth would not have been transmitted to future generations.[38]

Cut from a cloth splashed in blood, the nucleus narrative of *Sunrise Over Hell*[39], Ka-Tzetnik's first novel takes place in the Ghetto and Auschwitz and tells the story of Harry Preselshnik, the author's alter ego (this fact is undisputed—in the book, Harry is given the same inmate number that the

---

35   Gershon Shoffman, *The Complete Writings of G. Shoffman*, vol. 4 (Tel Aviv: Am Oved, 1962), 15.
36   Yehiel Szeintuch, *Ka-Tzetnik 135633: A Series of Dialogues with Yehiel Dinur* (Jerusalem: Beit Lochamei Hagetaot/Dov Sadan Institute, 2003), 126.
37   Ka-Tzetnik, *Ha-Tzofen* [A Vision] (Tel Aviv: Hakibutz Hameuchad, 1987), 73.
38   Moredechai Ovadyahu, "Mesaper ha-Planeta ha-Shchora: Ka-Tzetnik (Yehiel Dinur)" [A Story-Teller from a Black Planet: Ka-Tzetnik (Yehiel Dinur)], in *Be-Sa'ar u-vi-Dmama: Demuyut be-Sifrutenu ha-Chadasha* [*In Storm and in Stillness: Personalities of Our New Literature*] (Tel Aviv: Alef, 1976).
39   Ka-Tzetnik, *Sunrise Over Hell*.

author adopted for his pseudonym, 135633). The time is 1939, just before World War II, and the place is Metropoli, Poland. Watching with dismay the surfacing of rampant anti-Semitism, the talented and brilliant musician senses the looming danger about to engulf Polish Jewry. For instance, walking home with his fiancée Sania Schmidt, he notices a neon sign on the main street that declaims "TO BUY JEWISH IS TREASON."[40] Earlier, he hears the account of an esteemed mathematics professor Julian Stroitzki who is attacked by a gang of students, beaten and has the words "Leprous Jew to Palestine"[41] painted on his back. In response, Harry decides to immigrate to Palestine, where his future father-in-law, Schmidt, has settled. However, when the elderly industrialist hears of Harry's plans, he informs him through a letter that better he drowns his daughter in the sea than bring her to the inhospitable land. Reluctantly, the Zionist Harry agrees.

Ka-Tzetnik deftly shades in the prevailing mood among the Jewish community, using a gaggle of characters drawn from the arts and business, with each persona an archetypal representation of the various societal postures that existed at the time. We should not forget that since Dinur was armed with first-hand knowledge, he was able to vividly paint a historical portraiture interwoven with the personal tale of Sania and Harry that is mesmerizing in its eye for details and breadth of realism.

The narrative then surges headlong into the world of the irrational and the grotesque as the Germans invade Metropoli, rounding up Jews in the street, burning books and prayer shawls, and throwing into the fire beards that have been torn off the men's faces. Before long, the Jewish councils are created, followed by the establishment of the Ghetto. The author shows the wretched, imprisoned existence of slavery, humiliation and public executions in the ghetto, as well as the extreme starvation in the work camp to which Harry is transferred. Arriving at a labor camp in Germany, Harry is struck by the thousands of bony men, heads shaven and protruding jawbones greeting the newcomers with a plea for bread. In a telling moment, Harry tells himself that he is in another world. Later, the staggering, wrenching horror wrought by the Shoah is emblemized in a scene that involves Harry discovering the dead body of a friend, Marcel, next to the camp clinic, "Marcel's carcase-face, revealed to him the true face of man in the image of God. He bent, stretched out his hand and caressed the head of the Twentieth Century."[42]

---

[40] Ibid., 11.
[41] Ibid., 11.
[42] Ibid., 111.

Such sentiments haunt Ka-Tzetnik's pages, most notably the silence of heaven and the collapse of faith. The belief in the divine is ceaselessly shaken in view of the mountains of ritual prayer objects, the cutting of beards and forelocks, and the liquidation of pious Jews. An inmate whose entire family has been transported to the killing centers looks up at the sky and asks God if these atrocities are the reward for praising and extolling his name.And when Harry picks up a body and carries it to the mound of corpses, he turns it upside down since, "The image in the shape of this one Musselman, Heaven is not entitled to see."[43] In other words, a God that has allowed a Jew to reach such severe emaciation and fate is not entitled to see the individual's face.

Ultimately, Harry is transported to Auschwitz without Sania, where he is assigned the duty of removing the gold teeth from the mouths of the charred corpses. The arrival at Auschwitz signifies the end of the journey and of life: "The train arrived on the new planet. The doors were shoved apart and humanity drained out of the cattle trucks onto the vast platform."[44] At one point, a prisoner asks if there is a life in Auschwitz, to which another responds, "Anyone wanting to live here' got to kill somebody else…"[45] Later, we read, "…all were in one image, and dispossessed of the last distinguishing mark brought along from the other world—the individual name. Harry Preleshnik, no longer Harry Preleshnik, but turned into a number, was one of the a collective kind, one of a collective name—Ka-Tzetnik."[46]

In addition to the daily savagery, there are also the *Musselmen*—those emaciated, half-dead prisoners who are the touchstone, the reflexive marker for the unsettling dehumanization at Auschwitz. Unable to eat or feel hunger, the *Musselmen* eject any food that they ingest because of their ravaged intestine and are immediately dispatched to the gas chambers once identified by the camp doctor. Unsurprisingly, at one point, Harry is reduced to the state of the *Musselman*, joining the row of the totally skeletonized group marching to the crematorium. Yet, he is able to draw on his last nugget of internal strength and attempt escape. Although captured, the SS men, impressed by his daring act, decide to spare him immediate death and send him back to work. In another book, *Shivitti*, Dinur says to a Rabbi whom he sees in a vision, "At last you must admit, Rabbi, that God of the Diaspora himself is climbing into this truck—a Muselman."[47]

---

43   Ibid., 181.
44   Ibid., 158.
45   Ibid., 161.
46   Ibid., 161-162.
47   Ka-Tzetnik, *Shivitti: A Vision*, 7.

Sunrise Over Hell accentuates the notion of love, glaringly absent among the chimneys of Auschwitz, through the Harry and Sania relationship. Against incredible odds, the couple manages to remain devoted to each other in spite of the fact that they are separated and can only communicate through a fragmented exchange of letters. It is fairly evident that Sania carries a deep sense of guilt for not listening to her father and not leaving for Palestine; it is this feeling that guides her actions. To be sure, she sees herself responsible for the fate that befalls Harry. As the story develops, Sania saves Harry from a certain death by storming into a government office demanding his release from a labor camp, and Harry refuses a friend's offer to smuggle him out of the country, opting instead to remain with Sania.

Significantly, in complete opposition to the stereotypical and false image of the Diaspora Jew held by many Israelis in the 1950s, the author repeatedly overscores Sania's heroism, adumbrating her as the exemplar of the proud Jew, suffused with dignity and strength, constantly on guard for her loved ones, and unwilling to bend to Nazi rule. In fact, she is the one who fights in the Warsaw Ghetto uprising and later joins the partisans. Indeed, throughout the book, her fierce determination to fight rather than surrender is on display front and center. For instance, she tells Rabbi Frumkin, who opposes armed resistance, that while he has chosen for himself and disciples a shameful death, she and her comrades are sanctifying the name of Israel,

> We are idolators each time we run, like rats, to hide in our holes and see our children led off to be burnt in sacrifice to Moloch! Idolators, an understatement. We're worse—profaners, blasphemers of the name of Israel!... But while you prefer a death of shame for you and your kind, we have chosen to sanctify the name of Israel, and to write the history of the Ghetto rebellion with our blood. No, it isn't you, Rabbi, but we are acting in accordance with the law of Israel and in the name of God.[48]

In the end, Sania is ultimately trapped by a Gestapo operative after boarding a train destined for Auschwitz that she believes is headed for Switzerland. Thrust into the belly of the beast, Sania quickly becomes a *Musselman* and is discovered by Harry, who recognizes his wife's corpse by the mole on her cheek. Given her construction as a woman of valor and the fact that throughout the tale she is drawn as a woman of action who is able to elude the Nazis time and again and who defies her inevitable fate with all the cunning she can muster, Sania's death is all the more shocking because

---

48 Ibid., 195.

of the state she is found in and the fact that it is the gentle, passive Harry who endures. Above all, Harry survives the annihilating smokestacks so he can testify to the truth and relate the calamity to those who were not there. It is only then, according to the author, that we can truly and tangibly incubate the dead in our memory and in our soul.

Author Gershon Shoffman wrote that *Beit ha-Bubot* (*House of Dolls*) is a holy book.[49] In fact, so moved were the King of Denmark and the Queen of Belgium by the book that they wrote to Ka-Tzetnik's wife to convey their appreciation and respect. Certainly, the most famous and widely read of his novels, *House of Dolls* centers on a young Jewish girl, Daniella Preselshnik—in reality, the writer's sister, also named Daniella. Three days before the outbreak of World War II, the fourteen-year-old is captured in Poland while on a trip at the end of the school year and is transferred to a Nazi women's camp, the ironically named "Camp Labor Via Joy," where she is forced to become a prostitute for the German soldiers. The plot is based on the notebook kept by Daniella of her own experiences in the camp.

Told in flashback, the narrator is Harry, Daniella's brother, who is assigned to the sick bay, although he had never graduated medical school and although there are no medicines, no beds, no instruments, and—most important—no patients. Instead, he is charged with overseeing the burial of the piles of Jewish bodies, all the while struggling not to surrender to the impending debasement of life that turns those interned into *Musselmen*—shadow men. As discussed earlier in this chapter, these are the deformed, crippled, near dead human skeletons, who are the embodiment of human misery and lost hope. Over the course of the novel, Harry loses all those who are close to him, including his friend Tedek, once a member of the Ghetto resistance, who is now enamored of Daniella.

As the girls enter the camp and are directed to their division, they are first sterilized and then inducted into the abhorrent master–slave relationship of the "House of Dolls" for which they are simply not prepared. The extreme sexual abuse and their treatment as mere objects in this brothel limpidly illustrates the familiar trope of Ka-Tzetnik's series of novels—the Holocaust as the most horrifying, obscene, and unique of modern situations.[50] We learn, for instance, that the "dolls" must be in perfect physical condition for the visiting soldiers en route to the Russian front, or for those coming from the transit terminus, who stop by to prey upon the weak and vulnerable Jewesses. In addition, the discovery of any venereal infection means immediate doom, for any damage results in transportation to the ovens. Worse,

---

49 Shoffman, *The Complete Writings*, 28.
50 Yosef Heftman, "Beit ha-Bubot" ["The House of Dolls"], *Ha-Boker*, April 19, 1953, 6

if the concentration camp guards or other "German warriors" leave unsatisfied with their entertainment, they only need to convey their displeasure and report the number tattooed on the girl's breast. In the event that three such complaints are recorded, death is instant. Over and over, the tale is intent on exceedingly reinforcing and reminding us that within the framework of the barracks, every act led to the distortion and the elimination of life. To take but one example: when the new girls arrive, the veteran girls know that soon a selection will follow to replace those whose bodies have deteriorated. In effect, the newcomers are their executioners.

In a similar vein, we read that every girl must smile to show her appreciation of the pervasive cruelty meted out day and night, knowing that her life depends on seeming happy and content for the "guests." One could venture the observation that in portraying such events and situations, there exists the risk of triviality and objectionable eroticism, of seducing the reader to voyeuristically participate in the sexual victimization presented rather than focus on the horror perpetrated.

Still, it is equally clear that, on a different reading, the text does gravitate to that other central theme hovering above—the strength of the women-victims to spiritually survive the gory dehumanization by the Nazis in spite of the beatings and rape. In fact, there are various instances of the will to live and to preserve one's sanity and dignity that can be found in the book. One is the tale of Tzevia, an orthodox girl from the religious seminary of *Beit Ya'akov* who purposefully and stubbornly refuses to acquiesce to her tormentors' repulsive demands, though she knows the result of such repudiation. Thus, inevitably, Tzevia is bludgeoned to death, standing naked in the execution arena, defiant and strong, admirably victorious in keeping her chasteness and virtue whole. Another striking case in point is Daniella, who keeps her head up and who, against the odds, upholds her moral integrity.

As the novel draws to a close, the heroine seeks to escape her dreaded existence. She demonstrates her active resistance by walking toward the barbed wire fence, fully aware that she will be executed. Beforehand, she begs her friend to pass on her locket and notebook to her brother. Not surprisingly, she is shot by an SS sentry who knows he will be rewarded with three days leave for ending her bid for freedom. Following the murder, the guard bursts out singing, intoxicated with euphoria, aware that tomorrow he is going to his family and to his only daughter, whom he misses so desperately.

The dark, violent barbarism of the German officers knows no bounds. A panoply of abominations abounds. Elsewhere, the same sentry clobbers

Tzevia's sister Hanna to death, in a methodical, gut wrenching display. To the pious woman's shouts of "God all mighty, save me," he responds with well-directed and vicious blows to her head, legs, arms, and ankles. He then watches calmly as she writhes in pain, plunges her teeth into the ground, and tears her hair out. Afterwards, he coolly rests to devour his sandwich. Then, there are the medical experiments conducted on the girls by the German professor, including artificial inseminations, tests on twins, coerced abortions and sterilizations, or the raw cruelty of Elsa, the brothel overseer.

Significantly, Daniella's family photographs, the only means she has to recreate the safe childhood she still clings to, are destroyed upon her entering the camp, foregrounding the callousness of the Nazis and their desire to deprive the prisoners of any emotional ties to their former life. Indeed, they succeed in obliterating every remnant of the past. Early on, it is revealed that old photographs fall to the floor of the cutting room where the young women work, ripping the seams of the garments taken from the victims in search of anything hidden. The scattered pictures, some of brides and grooms, some of babies in their cribs, are stepped on and swept into the rubbish heap.

While the narrative describes Daniella's, Harry's, and the other inmates' ordeals and sexual exploitation in graphic detail, Ka-Tzetnik ensures that the teenager's memories of family, love, and tradition—engraved deeply in her psyche—are not erased. To wit, as a counterpoint, the author undercuts his sequences of sheer Dantean hell with the quotidian innocence and loyalty that typified the life of Daniella and her brother in the town of Kongressia before the war. Among other things, this serves to further underscore the nauseating degradation they are subjected to and to emphasize the two realities, each as stridently polar as the other.

Compositionally, Ka-Tzetnik employs flashbacks to paint life in the ghetto as well as the mass deportations, eerily shading in the pitiful images and mood of the destitute and condemned residents, sent by the Judenrat councillors to the killing centers, who favor the rich over the poor in their selection of the daily quota. It is also abundantly evident that the rabid anti-Semitism not only emanates from the Nazis but also from the Polish peasants and partisans. At one point, Daniella, fleeing from a carnage of her school friends in the Yablova market, pleads with a Polish farmer to take her in but is told to get out. In the same breath, she kisses the hands of the farmer's daughter, hoping she can convince her father to have mercy on the little Jewess begging for help, but to no avail.

Through the succession of vignettes accompanied by interior monologues, Ka-Tzetnik pulls the reader into Daniella's world, dramatizing and compounding the sadism to which the protagonist must adapt, but ultimately cannot. Interestingly, the scenes of battery and psychical defilements are inscribed in a nonjudgmental, neutral manner, perhaps as a tacit acknowledgment that what is being chronicled is appropriately described in objective mode since the satanic acts speak volumes and do not require the subjective.

In his book *The Seventh Million*, Tom Segev writes: "I was a boy when I first read *Qaru Lo Piepel* (the original Hebrew title of *Atrocity*). I have never read anything about the Holocaust that so disturbed me."[51] More striking is author and newspaper editor Haim Shorer's 1961 plea to Gideon Hausner, the state prosecutor in the Eichmann Trial:

> Leave aside your concluding speech and take Ka-Tzetnik's latest book *Piepel* and read it out loud to the court and to its listeners and don't stop…Read in a loud voice and we will listen and cry for two–three days and nights. All of us, all of Israel, we will cry and wail without end; perhaps we could wipe away with the sea of tears the great horror, whose depth we yet not know. We will cry until we faint with our dear Ka-Tzetnik, with his pure and holy book.[52]

Likewise, the 1961 book's English version contained on its jacket a quote from a reviewer, who noted the following: "The author regards himself as the keeper of a chronicle. Indeed, the essential importance of the book is its documentary side, second to which is its literary rendering. It is the very documentation which I see as a major literary achievement."[53]

A layered mosaic of unimaginable, inconceivably traumatic vignettes, the main subject of *Atrocity*, the final instalment of the trilogy that began with *Sunrise over Hell*, is the sexual exploitation of children in the concentration camps. The nub of the narrative follows Moni, the seven-year-old boy who is forced to become a child prostitute, a *Piepel*, to serve the needs of the older guards and section orderlies. First appearing in *House of Dolls*, the naïf, tender, and refined child, modelled after the author's own brother, arrives at Auschwitz and is immediately noticed by block ruler Franzel because of his apparently tempting gentle eyes.

Traversing familiar territory, Ka-Tzetnik manages to brilliantly transcribe, from the perspective of a youthful hero, the horrifying crimes committed against children in the Holocaust and to embed the story's fabric

---

51 Segev, *The Seventh Million*, 5.
52 Haim Shorer, "To the Prosecutor in the Eichmann Trial: About a Terrible and Holy Book," *Davar*, June 1961, 21.
53 Quoted in Yuter, *The Holocaust in Hebrew Literature*, 5.

with illuminating insights about the torture and destruction of innocent lives. At its epicenter, the book is a rites of passage tale, unfolding in an insane universe, where cruelty and subjugation go hand in hand. Further, the story is also about the struggle of children to grasp the intolerable reality they are thrust into, and to behave heroically in a corrupt, abnormal world. In many respects, *Atrocity*'s keynote theme is Moni's attempt to preserve his sanity and integrity even as he is ceaselessly preyed upon by the vicious, evil men of the block.[54]

Looming heavily among the pages of *Atrocity* are consuming images of the sadistic debasement of human life that chillingly flash throughout. In one disturbing passage, Fruchtenbaum, a Jew and scion of a Zionist family who was once a *Piepel* and now runs one of the blocks, hacks to death a fellow Jew for recognizing him and reminding him of his suppressed heritage. Repeatedly, Ka-Tzetnik hammers home the idea that perversity and murder were polymorphous in the Nazi phenomenon and could turn the son of a renowned Jewish leader into a brutal, cruel man. Furthermore, he stresses that the camp inmates, in their abject existence, would do anything to survive, even if it involved violence against their brethren.

This clearly underscores Ka-Tzetnik's core tenor—that Auschwitz was a planet separate from the rest of the world, a place where one could not be good, where one had to reverse traditional morality and act with total callousness. The survival instinct looms large in a terrifying catalogue of scenes: a Nazi officer chokes a young boy to death after his rape; an old *Piepel* is seesawed from side to side with a cane laid across his neck; a cell block master smothers one of his captives by pushing his head into the latrine hole; an adolescent is punished with death for stealing jam for the Rabbi, who yearns for the sweet taste.

In common with Ka-Tzetnik's other texts, the *Musselmen* once again comprise a central part of the symbology of depravity and expunction of life. The *Musselmen* relate to one of the operating themes in the author's work—namely, that of re-creation, or miscreation, as Howard Needler puts it.[55] In Ka-Tzetnik, we are presented with the deformed creation of man in the form of the *Musselman,* the walking dead, whose very existence represents a reversal of the vision described in Genesis. Needler observes that,

---

54 Tzvika Dror, "Ve-ha-Siyut Sholet Bo: Mifalo ha-Sifruti-Te'udi shel Ka-Tzetnik," [And the Nightmare Dominates Him: the Literary-Documentary Legacy of Ka-Tzetnik], *Davar*, April 20, 1990.
55 Howard Needler, "Red Fire Upon Black Fire: Hebrew in the Holocaust Novels of K. Tsetnik," in *Writing in the Holocaust*, ed. Berel Lang (New York: Holmes and Meier, 1988), 241-42.

"Instead of being in the 'image of God', we have a creature from whom the image of man has been all but effaced."[56] The *Musselmen*, sardonically and grotesquely labelled by the author as the flower of the twentieth century, are the result of Nazi transmogrification.

At one point, Moni, escaping the unprecedented savagery of block chief Robert, seeks shelter among the *Musselmen* and is hardly noticed by the men who have had any trace of life snuffed out by the debauchery of their enslavers. Notably, the *Musselmen* are entrusted with safeguarding the food rations, for it is known that their desire to eat has dissipated and that that they no longer possess any consciousness of their surroundings. Above all, the blank, hollowed out, spiritually emaciated corpses slowly crawling toward their liberating death personify the surreal and subhuman depths a person can be reduced to.

As to be expected, Moni's odyssey into the netherworld is explicitly charted, emphasizing his inability to shake off the fetters of his Judaic past. Moni is acutely aware of the fate that awaits him if he allows those values to surface, as they are in direct opposition to the demands of Robert. For instance, Moni refuses to eat, though he has access to all the food he craves, and though he knows that these acts will surely lead to death, for his tormentors like their sexual objects to be of supple and round flesh. Inevitably, the sensitive young protagonist, who longs for his parents, grows too thin to continue his function as a *Piepel* and is replaced by Lolek. Still, he cannot hate his substitute, because he believes that Lolek—just like he does—yearns to see his mother, who is interned at the women's camp. Indeed, despite the relentless suffering and pervasive anguish around him, Moni never loses his humanity. We reflect, for instance, that he embraces the Talmudic teachings of The Rabbi of Shilov, who, through his Yom Kippur prayer and mere presence in the camp, is able to infuse Moni's wretched existence with a modicum of meaning and hope.

As with other Ka-Tzetnik novels, there is no redemptive end. After stealing a turnip and receiving a ruthless beating for his "sin," Moni finds release when he valiantly attempts to escape by lunging at the barbed wire. Significantly, his brave, life-affirming act elicits unexpected praise from block chief Robert, and from Vatzek, a German Kapo, who recognize his courageous refusal to succumb to the impending death from starvation that awaits the others. Perhaps the deepest message of the book is that it is only in the world of Auschwitz, where all values had been so overtly inverted, where all moral prescriptions were eclipsed by ritualized monstrosity,

---

56   Needler, "Red Fire Upon Black Fire," 241.

where the usual distinctions between right and wrong vanished, that the death of a little boy is preferable to life.

In different ways, Ka-Tzetnik's 1960 *Ha-Shaon Asher Me'al Ha-Rosh* (in English translation, *Star Eternal*) is a remarkable, seminal achievement in the Holocaust canon, lauded by John K. Roth as one of the, "unrivalled gems of Holocaust literature."[57] According to a new biography, then Israeli Prime Minister Menachem Begin, at a meeting convened prior to the 1981 air attack on the Iraqi nuclear reactor, referred to the clock ticking above their heads, quoting directly from the first pages of *Star Eternal*.[58] Moreover, the book was published as a special school edition and provided as a gift by the Israeli Ministry for Culture and Education to year 10 students.[59] The Israeli Defense Forces furnished its soldiers with a pocket-sized edition of the work.

At once a disturbing and edifying work, it depicts in vivid, yet simple and direct detail the unspeakable horrors of concentration camp existence, functioning as a summary of Ka-Tzetnik's thematic template. Above all, it describes the gruesome events of the "Final Solution" in a pared down, staccato style and language that tangibly pierce the impenetrable thick wall erected by readers that often prevents any cognitive or emotional engagement. Put simply, it arouses and extracts a deep chill of empathy and shock from the spectator and, in the process, opens a window for future generations to allow them to connect with the world of the Holocaust.

Star Eternal possesses a mimetic surface clarity, severely filleted, that is aided and abetted by the brevity of the basic Hebrew, pruned of metaphor and hyperbole. Laconic, trimmed, and controlled, its effect is so natural that the bewildered reader is increasingly unaware of how much detail is being described. For example, a scene that conveys the twisted reality that in the death camp a day begins at night is typically compressed: "Naked march into the night. Midnight silence of Auschwitz..."[60] Elsewhere, forcible labour is thus limned, "With every thrust of your spade you bury the sun in the earth."[61] Likewise, when Harry Preselshnik attempts to verbalize his torment at Auschwitz, he plainly remarks, "Words are no more."[62] Elsewhere,

---

57   John K. Roth, "On Seeing the Invisible Dimensions of the Holocaust," *Holocaust and Genocide Studies* 1, no. 1 (1986): 149.
58   Jason Warshof, "The Begin Phenomenon," *Jerusalem Post*, May 4, 2015, 14.
59   Aderet, "Professor Gideon Greif Nilcham 'al Kvodo ha-'Avud shel Ka-Tzetnik."
60   Ka-Tzetnik 135633, *Star Eternal* (London: W. H. Allen, 1972), 39.
61   Ibid., 17.
62   Ibid., 41.

forced labor is thus described, "With every thrust of your spade you bury the sun in the earth."[63]

Admittedly, the conflation of razor-sharp sentences with fragmented descriptions underscores the author's desire to reflect the crushed, disjointed reality that is outside any normative framework and which does not fit into any logical, coherent mold. Hence, it is not unreasonable to suggest that the message foisted upon the audience is that here is a perverted reality, stripped bare of the conventional constituents of time and space.

Originally published in Hebrew under the title *The Clock*, it is small wonder that the central operating motif that informs *Star Eternal* is that of time and, more specifically, the parallel time frames of normal Europe, where people live typical, ordinary lives, and "Planet Auschwitz," where Jews suffer terror and inhumanity. The book is made up of a series of jarring, loosely coupled episodes, which the author calls "stages." Each chapter is self-contained, encasing within its midst a separate title and storyline, and pivots around disparate threads of camp living—leavened, for the most part, by a welter of jolts, gnomic words, and twists.

Bookended by a prologue and epilogue, *Star Eternal* begins in the narrator's eerily quiet street, bathed in the searing heat of the sun and featuring a boulevard of display windows. The author adumbrates the tranquillity of the place, heightened by snippets of banality peppered throughout the opening pages, and then quickly dismantles it in revealing the date: September 9, 1939, the day when Hitler's army marched into Poland, marking the start of World War II.

It is then that humanity's cultural clock reverts to zero, when the sand hour suddenly trickles to a different, one is tempted to say, otherworldly beat. Even more starkly, the city's electric clock is in synchronicity with the unfolding of events— its hands rest on 9 A.M. Thus, we have an application of a direct and realistic portraiture, devoted to the profound and sober chronicling of a specific place and time, setting down a visage of the "other planet," to borrow from Ka-Tzetnik once more, in precise detail and lineament.

After the hero, Ferber, is taken to Auschwitz, the narrative lens zeroes in on this world with uncompromising eyes, capturing with perfectly modulated metrics the indigestible tableau, images of annihilation and the doing of evil that defies description. With a raw filmic gaze, the author, possessing such a strong grip on his material, leads the reader into the vertex of Auschwitz, into the black hole, condensing into a few passages the feeling

---

63   Ibid., 17.

of omnipresent death. As the narrative is written in the second person, the reader is addressed openly and is thus positioned to see the inmate's world, and is co-opted into participating in an experience from which, by reason of distance, they are explicitly excluded. In other words, the reader is invited to adopt and comply with the mood, vulnerability and torment that the shaping of the plot seeks to present.

There are moments of uninhibited infernal magnitude. In one episode, we step into the "showers," surrounded by the bony, living dead, and stare into the sprinklers above our head in anticipation for the stream of Zyklon B to spurt blue gas into our lungs. The graphic and bluntly testimonial description of the "inner sanctum of the Temple of Auschwitz,"[64] with its concrete details, transports the reader into the "ground zero" of the camps, into the gas chambers like never before, is terrifying:

> A wisp of white steam. Unhurrying. Leisurely. Lightly twisting and weaving. Gracefully curling against the sprinkler pores as if circling a floor in dance… Shower pores of the Auschwitz "Bath House". Suddenly: Thin, freezing streaks. Biting whips of frost. A moment—and off they break in mid-air. Gone… All at once a wailing shriek crashes out: "Water!!! Man—Water!!!" Necks suddenly beget heads—heads with eyes; heads with mouths… Bodies leap into the air, howling and screaming, tearing their scalps as they would tear hair.[65]

In another, we join the column of men the author names *Musselmen*, the nearly dead skeletons, standing crowded among the block walls, trembling in fear of the camp commander who may arbitrarily sentence anyone to death. In yet another, the reader shudders while joining the roll call of prisoners lined up for selection to the crematorium, hoping against hope that they will be overlooked. If anything, the unflagging pace, the leaping from one visceral episode of agonizing torture to another, the repeated catalogue of atrocities presented in explicit specificity, are all chokingly disturbing. One need only consider a sequence in which a group lunges at the ground to lick the remains of some spilled soup, one's teeth biting into the other, to understand the reduction of the human condition to its most basic level depicted here.

There are many other such incidents that dapple the book. A man is set to be beaten to death for attempting to obtain another plate of soup, or because he urinated during a curfew, and is then mercilessly killed; a row

---

64   Ibid., 44.
65   Ibid, 45-46.

of musicians, made up of Europe's most talented and gifted, accompanying those sentenced into the chambers, play in thunderous tones to silence the wailing of those who cannot bear their fate; a Jew digs with his own hands a mass grave for his brethren about to be shot.

And still, in the midst of the machinery of death, a note of optimism for the future can be drawn from a striking theological conversation between Ferber and the Rabbi of Shilev, titled "The Last Argument." At one point, Ferber ponders the question of the Jewish people's destiny, asking the Rabbi why God has deserted his children and delivered them to the hands of the beast. He goes further, likening the Almighty to a walking dead, "Admit now, Rabbi of Shilev, God of the Diaspora Himself flounders here in this snarl of bones—a Musselman!"[66] In response, the Rabbi states that out of the ruins and ashes of the night, the nation of Israel will rise in the Promised Land with its eternal star brightly shining. On the face of it, false hope. Yet, for our hero, a nourishing vision.

At the novel's conclusion, when the main protagonist returns from Auschwitz to his hometown, Metropoli, the same clock has not stood still but is still running. Only this time, it is a transformed place that he encounters. "And over his head the same "Electra" clock. But his time has lost all connection with him. His time had broken out of its ambits, and runs on the cogwheels of a different world."[67] Ferber is a changed man: "He stood, a denizen fallen from a foreign planet… skull shaven bare, a skeleton in the stripped shreds of the Ka-Tzet uniform."[68] We are reminded of the evil and cruelty that still lurks beneath the surface of civilised folks as the townspeople ignore him, shutting the doors in the very houses in which the dead Jews used to live. A compendium of the devastating effects of the camp is supplied in the text's concluding lines. Here, Ferber pleads that one hair of his sister's golden locks be returned, along with one of his father's shoes, and one wheel of his brother's bicycle, "Give me—give me back one single hair of my sister's golden curls! Give me back one shoe of my father's; A broken wheel from my little brother's skates; And a mote of dust that on my mother rested—"[69]

---

66 Ibid, 113.
67 Ibid, 115.
68 Ibid, 114-115.
69 Ibid, 126.

Chapter 6

A Funny and Sensitive Story about Holocaust Memory in Israel

It is hardly surprising that the story "Shoes," by Etgar Keret, which forms the basis for this chapter, was published in Israel of the 1990s. As the era of first-generation stories slowly reached its terminus, it was in the 1980s and 1990s that vigorous second-generation Holocaust fiction came of age as a genre of indirect cultural memory and matured into a fully fledged literary category as authors began to add their unique voice to this weighty and painful subject matter. Haunted by what happened to the Jews at a time before they were born, though not possessing personal testimony to this new constituency, descendants and nondescendants were unrestrained by the constraints and taboos that shackled their predecessors in making art out of the atrocity. Today, this outpouring continues unabated.

Motivated by a powerful impulse to keep the Shoah legacy alive and unforgettable—and to honor the memory of the apocalypse—their literary response and engagement with the Holocaust often subverted or reoriented norms and narrative boundaries in exploring the enduring impact of this tragedy, and explored the national and universal lessons that could be learned. Taking the Shoah beyond the war, they situate their themes in a broader context as well as wrestling with the task of writing adequately about the catastrophe that engulfed European Jewry. Treating it as a vicarious past meant that these artists, though struggling with the impossibility of words to communicate the lingering questions and effect of the Holocaust, showed that the attempt must be made. Their passionate writing becomes even more timely and necessary given that, in the near future, they will be the critical sources in educating and transmitting the memories and knowledge of the survivors.

To be sure, the overwhelming sense that permeates second-generation engagement with the Holocaust is that as the survivors grow old and their numbers dwindle, their legacy and experiences have much to teach us and cannot be ignored: "With distance—and doubtless imitations—has come the ability to confront at last the ugly, cruel and contagious abandonment of morality that erupted in the middle of the century and of a civilisation emblematic of human progress," Gerald Jacobs writes, "with distance, too has come a willingness to engage the creative imagination with that same period of history in order to search for meaning, warning or consolation."[1]

Temporally removed from Hitler's war on the Jews, Israeli litterateurs offered different vantage points and angles in mourning those they did not know, and pushing back the crippling fetters of the chasm that yawns between the ever-incomprehensible catastrophe and their own biography. Struggling with questions of identity, faith, and God and the appropriate frames for remembrance, they have contributed—through a variety of voices, perspectives, and creative imagery—to a body of work that details the anguish of the sons and daughters of survivors or Israelis growing up in a post-Shoah Israel. Invariably, probing these energetic, often wildly creative and powerful constructions of the Shoah reminds us that writing about this calamity gnaws at the very heart of speaking about it. In not avoiding the pain of the past or participating in the process of any suppression, the next generation reminds contemporary society of the function of memory and its vital role.

In several ways, second-generation texts serve as testament to the fact that within Israeli and Jewish culture, literary representations of the Holocaust have transcended generational, tribal, or national limitations. Above all, it allows the reader to imagine what happened and allows the author to bring facts of the Holocaust to life with stunning intensity in a way that ideology and philosophical abstractions cannot. If before, the state was the storehouse of aggregate memory, enlisting its institutions in service of a singular narrative that dictated the terms for local memory of a specific experience—the Holocaust—this debilitating coherence no longer exists. In fact, the idea of an indisputable version or narrative has been challenged and absolutely dismantled.

No doubt, the psychological legacy is a key theme of the second-generation corpus. Rather than a focus on the grand theological or philosophical questions about the Shoah, writers zero in on

---

1 Gerald Jacobs, "The Jewish Literary Quarterly Awards," *Jewish Quarterly* 45, no. 1 (1998): 67.

...areas that a young Israeli writer can approach directly and faithfully on the basis of his authentic life experience...how are echoes of the Holocaust audible in Israeli life today, especially in the lives of young people? Do the children of survivors undergo some special experience different from their peers? What does the survivor generation look like to the children?[2]

Holocaust literature of the second generation has been labelled a "call to the imagination of a people to repair the work of reality—to recreate a destroyed world by infusing meaning into the very events that destroyed it—what else could be more moving?"[3] The power of stories written by those called "witnesses through the imagination" is that they furnish readers with the keys of awakening and experiencing the trauma their forebears experienced. Put differently, it is precisely because novelists produce meaning by connecting and linking things, in the context of the Holocaust, that fiction is able to communicate and broaden the Jewish experience in a profound, yet sensitive way. It is for that reason that one must not resist creatively tackling the topic of the Holocaust despite the obstacles strewn along that journey. As one critic notes, writers and readers alike must make available a space in their consciousness for the "second life" that stirs in our soul when we encounter the intense images of that event "so that we can move as far as it is given to us to do so, into the pain and hence the meaning of the Holocaust—that, too, is a kind of memorial."[4]

In considering the broad stylistic spectrum by the post-war group of Israeli novelists, one must probe the devices and tropes employed in such figurations of writing. Involved in this undertaking is a focus on ethical concerns related to such responses. The reason is that the outflow of Shoah writings, with its admixture of stylistic fiddling and new modes, seems to "test implicit boundaries and to raise not only aesthetic and intellectual problems, but moral issues too."[5] Doubtless, any attempt to enter this heart of darkness and to depict the destruction of European Jewry in belles lettres challenges "our traditional conceptual and representational categories."[6]

Current novelists must contend with the central paradox of crafting their stories from material that not only exists outside their own personal experience but also requires them to transcend their own reserves of imaginative

---

2   Avner Holtzman, "Trends in Israeli Holocaust Fiction in the 1980s," *Modern Hebrew Literature*, 8–9 (1992): 24–25.
3   Norma Rosen, *Accidents of Influence* (Albany, NY: State University of New York Press, 1992), 47.
4   Rosen, *Accidents of Influence*, 53.
5   Friedlander, "Trauma, Memory and Transference," 2, 3.
6   Ibid.

re-creation. Finding the proper modes of rewriting the unthinkable in modern literary terms and techniques remains an arduous challenge to the artist: "Holocaust reality limits rather than liberates the vision of the writer... who ventures to represent it. It abnormalizes the normal."[7]

Primarily, by confecting a story composed of authentic aspects and aesthetic inventions, and by plunging backwards to a time beyond their own life, authors risk the charge of tilting the genocidal reality to manipulate a reader's emotions. Indeed, the fictional constructs of secondhand cartographers, mapping out their own renderings (as the "bearing-witness" generation does) can transgress the sanctity of real events by rupturing their factual integrity—especially since they depend on the partaking of transmitted memory and mediated imagination. A related moral concern is whether wordsmiths who spin tales for their audience with the intended aim of moving and exciting the reader are benefiting from the victim's grief. A literary record of the Holocaust, set forth in heightened prose and with intense emotionalism, may indeed depend on the sensational and dramatic for its success.

Still, the positive effect of second-generation Holocaust literature cannot be understated:

> The stories... fulfil first and foremost a personal, mental need, a catharsis of the author. At the same time, however, they also satisfy collective needs... The stories... help and are helping, primarily, to change the personal, familial and national group of terms, from feelings of cowardice and offence to understanding and empathy of the situations of humiliation to which the victims were subjected and their sustaining of humanity at the very bottom... Instead of the shame, the repression, the reservations, a much better understanding of the parents' generation has developed, as well as an ability to identify with them...the stories have brought about not only an opening of a real dialogue with the parents' generation and the past, with the "there" and "then", but chiefly with ourselves. Through the works of the second generation, the terms "Jew" and "Israeli" assume their deep and profound meaning among the generation as a whole. The isolated personal memory of the past becomes a collective one, part of a combined Israeli and Jewish identity.[8]

---

7   Langer, *Preempting the Holocaust*, vii–xix.
8   Nurit Govrin, "Mavo'" [Introduction], in *Kova' Zechuchit* [*Hat of Glass*], ed. Nava Semel (Tel Aviv: Sifriyat Hapoalim, 1985), 9–10.

Born in Israel in 1967 to Polish survivors of what he once called "the black hole of the Holocaust,"[9] Etgar Keret's father survived "by living for almost 600 days in a 'hole in the ground' outside a village in Poland."[10] Keret has achieved acclaim as a short story writer, film director, and teacher of creative writing both in Israel and in the United States. His fiction has been described as magic realism and postmodernist, which simply means that he borrows from Kafka, Dante, and Kerouac, and blends the fantastical with everyday life. His great theme is the utter aloneness and alienation we all have felt at one time.

This wildly inventive author and creator of comics has managed to become a cultural icon and hero to a whole generation of Israelis, captivating the troubled nation with his razor sharp, subversive tales that sometimes run to only 50 words. His books have been translated into 42 languages, and his short stories routinely become best-sellers on release. They have also been adapted into 40 movies that have won the Israeli Oscar or garnered prizes from international film festivals.

Labelled as "The voice of Young Israel,"[11] Keret is such a literary celebrity that there are young writers mimicking his bag of bold writing tricks. Keret began writing as a journalist for local magazines; his first collection of stories—*Tzinorot* (*Pipelines*), published in 1992—became an instant best-seller. Subsequent books—such as *Ga'aguai le-Kissinger* (*Missing Kissinger*, 1992), *H-Keytana shel Kneller* (*Kneller's Happy Campers*, 1998) *Anihu* (*I Am*, 2002), *Pit'om Dfika ba-Delet* (*Suddenly, a Knock on the Door*, 2010), cemented his status as Israel's most successful postmodern writer. In 2016, he was awarded the Charles Bronfman Prize and the Italian Adei-Wizo Prize for his memoir *The Seven Good Years*.

Keret has hit a nerve with Israel's veteran writers, such as A. B. Yehoshua, who don't find his fast, tough prose, especially appealing. In fact, Yehoshua has attacked Keret's outrageous writing, saying that he avoids grappling with the big picture issues in favor of trendy urban self-analysis. But it would seem that Yehoshua refuses to accept that Keret is interested in people, rather than in the grand national questions. Keret believes he infuriates authors like Yehoshua because the Keret style "…doesn't derive from any

---

9 Alice O'Keeffe, "Etgar Keret: Israelis Boycott Me as a Traitor, and Foreigners Because I'm Israeli," The Guardian, August 1, 2015, accessed August 8, 2018, https://www.theguardian.com/books/2015/aug/01/etgar-keret-books-interview-israel-the-seven-good-years.
10 Ibid.
11 Linda Grant, "Etgar Keret: Life: Try it Some Time," *The Independent* (London), February 25, 2005.

Israeli tradition."[12] He adds, "I'm different from everything the mainstream here knows, and they don't know how to digest me. I don't think I am influenced by any canonized Israeli writer. Because they can't really connect to my writing, they refer to me in clichés."[13]

And though the literary establishment now regards his work as part of the Hebrew canon, Keret cares little for such recognition. It has not prevented him from winning the Prime Minister's Award for Literature or travelling to Poland with former Israeli President Shimon Peres to dedicate that country's newly established Holocaust Museum.

As a child of Holocaust survivors (his mother was a child in the Warsaw Ghetto), this unprecedented catastrophe naturally informs his writing. Growing up in Israel of the 1970s in the shadow of the Shoah and surrounded by the remnant that settled in the Jewish state, he says he felt "a crippling sense of insignificance"—his experience dwarfed by what his parents had endured, "'I would bump into a wall and I wouldn't cry, because I'd say, 'You just bumped into a wall. Smile to your mum and make her happy.'"[14] In another interview, he revealed that, "Everything I write, is a strange projection of my limited life experience."[15] Certainly, Keret has a tendency to focus on small, intimate details and marginal events in the life of a child or an ordinary person, limited by emotional immaturity or education, that illuminate weighty moral, ethical, or political problems.

As the international panel of judges noted in announcing Keret as the 2016 Charles Bronfman Prize recipient in recognition of his work conveying Jewish values across cultures and imparting a humanitarian vision throughout the world: "In a dangerous world, Etgar Keret portrays people who have the capacity to empathize with the other, to hear the other, and to find compassion for the other. He counters dehumanization and inspires his readers with warmth and humor and original thinking. He encourages others to make the world a better place and translates the lessons of the Holocaust to a new generation."[16]

---

12 Moshe Temkin, "One Happy Camper," *The Jerusalem Post*, March 29, 1999.
13 Ibid.
14 Ben Naparstek, "Interview with Etgar Keret," *Tikkun* 20, no. 5 (September/October 2005): 71.
15 Ryan Krull, "The Rumpus Interview with Etgar Keret," *Rumpus,* July 27, 2015, accessed August 8, 2018. http://therumpus.net/2015/07/the-rumpus-interview-with-etgar-keret/.
16 "The Charles Bronfman Prize Names Etgar Keret as 2016 Recipient," accessed August 8, 2018, https://thecharlesbronfmanprize.org/pressreleases/the-charles-bronfman-prize-names-etgar-keret-as-2016-recipient/.

It is from the collection of short tales, *Missing Kissinger*, that the story "Shoes"[17] is drawn, which forms our discussion here. Keret has expounded on the central import in "Shoes":

> It's a story about the difference between a mausoleum kind of memory and the memory that you own and is always with you. This is the kind of difference between the memory I have of the holocaust from my parents and the memory I have from school of the holocaust. My dad once said to me 'we had some horrible experiences, but the first time I ever kissed a girl was during these years. We live through these years, we didn't experience them as symbols, we had happy days sometimes, we didn't know that life could be better.'"[18]

In the same interview, Keret defended his employment of humor in dealing with a heavy subject such as the Holocaust: "If I don't use humour, I revert to pathos very easily," he says. "And the thing with pathos is that it is clichéd and it is not effective for communication and humour is a way of self-criticism, of showing that you are in the system but out of the system, it is two-tiered thinking."[19]

On another level, "Shoes" is meditation about the difficulty, or perhaps inability, of young Israelis to profoundly grasp their parents' and grandparents' Holocaust experience. It is no accident that Keret chose the title "Shoes" for a story about remembering the Holocaust in modern Israel. Shoes have become such an iconic and jarring artifact of the European genocide and the horror of the six million Jews murdered by the Nazis. One of the most sombre monuments on display at the Auschwitz death camp is a huge glass case that contains mounds of ownerless shoes that were once worn by the victims. The forlorn shoes are, literally and figuratively, a living testimony to the cruelty of the oppressors and the momentous responsibility that present generations have in bearing witness to the hallowed memory of the dead.

The story begins as the schoolboy narrator and his class visit the Museum of Volhynia Jewry as part of the annual pilgrimage to mark Holocaust Memorial Day. On the bus, the narrator reflects on who suffered more, East European or Oriental Jews, dramatizing the hierarchical claims to pain and victimhood that persist among Israelis, along the lines of ethnic

---

17 I am using the English translation to be found in Etgar Keret, *The Bus Driver Who Wanted to be God and Other Stories* (New York: Thomas Dunne, 2001).
18 Peter Lalor, "Twisted Reality Check," *The Daily Telegraph*, April 5, 2003.
19 Ibid.

and cultural background: "...I felt very important. All the kids in the class except me, my cousin, and another boy, Druckman, were of Iraqi origins. I was the only one with a grandfather who died in the Holocaust."[20] It is precisely this sense of uniqueness that spurs the young man to later touch a black-and-white cardboard photograph of a survivor.

The children are warned not to touch any of the exhibits, yet the boy violates that prohibition when he touches the photograph on the wall of a skinny old man. When a female classmate of the narrator points out her friend's transgression, he replies, in an angry tone and with proprietary conviction, that the picture is of his grandfather and therefore he is allowed to break the rules. It is therefore probable that already at the opening of the story the grandchild takes a particular interest in his ancestor, and may see in this photograph an emotion or detail about the Holocaust that all his parents' and teachers' comments hitherto have not been able to impart. It appears that the picture comes to represent the absent grandfather that he knows very little about since his mother is reluctant to speak about her dead father. We glimpse a sense of this discomfort when, a few weeks later, the mother mishandles—or perhaps purposely avoids—the opportunity to deepen the discussion about her father when the boy mentions him in relation to the shoes bought in Germany.

In asking whether the Museum of Volhynia Jewry symbolizes "tradition, the establishment, hegemonic culture, or the presence of the past in the future and our responsibility to the past,"[21] Roman Katzman asserts that the institution, in how it functions in the story, resembles more closely a "cemetery, an exhibition of deceased objects."[22] He then posits that the contact the young boy makes with the image is the first step in "...reviving the objects. The caressing of the photograph is a childish, naïve gesture, but at the same time it is an ethereal flash of ethics...this touch means accepting responsibility and accepting the face of the old man."[23] Katzman further maintains that through that simple, moral act, the boy imbues the past with a new meaning, divorced from the hierarchy of the museum and the multitude of artifacts placed on its shelves. It is not unreasonable to argue that only by ignoring the official rules of the museum and its ritualistic, abstract ceremony—which does not awaken or generate any empathy—and by breaking

---

20 Keret, "Shoes," 55.
21 Roman Katzman, "Ga 'aguim le-Mitos: 'Ishiyut, 'Etica, ve-'Ideologia ba-Mitopoesis shel Etgar Keret" [Longing for Myth: Personality, Ethics, and Ideology in the Mythopoesis of Etgar Keret], *Mikan* 4 (January 2005): 21.
22 Ibid.
23 Ibid.

the reverential and petrifying rules imposed by the state, that the boy finds the route to bond and identify with the victims. In many ways, Keret rejects the rigid boundaries of statist memory in favor of personal memory. In that context, the author has responded to critics who have accused him of treating the Holocaust with disrespect by declaring, "It's not your memory; it doesn't belong to the nation. It belongs to me."[24]

After the screening of a movie showing Jewish children pushed into a truck and gassed, the students are introduced to a survivor who has been invited to testify about his ordeal. The old man pleads with the students not to buy German goods since, "…underneath the fancy wrapping there are parts and tubes that they made of the bones and skin and flesh of dead Jews."[25] As he listens to the speech by the former concentration camp inmate, the young man embraces the plea by the old man, flavoring his ruminations with deadpan humor: "…I thought to myself it was lucky we had a made-in-Israel refrigerator at home. Why look for trouble?"[26] It is of note that within the confines of the museum, the school students are twice issued with a negative imperative: first, not to touch any of the exhibits on display and then, not to purchase German-made products.

Two weeks later, his parents, who have returned from an overseas trip, have bought him a pair of German *Adidas* sneakers. Throughout, Keret remains nonjudgmental, as we come to sympathize with the young hero. The perspective is comical when the young narrator feels superior to his second-generation parents and his older brother, since the purchase of the shoes seems to indicate to him that these authority figures in his life are unaware of the truth revealed in the memorial speech by the guest speaker.

To be sure, the narrator is utterly convincing and sincere in his quest to keep the memory of the Holocaust alive and to honor the survivor's plea. At first, he takes issue with the present, shrewdly attempting to remind his mother about the origins of the shoes, hoping that he can manage to avoid wearing the sneakers and to stir within his mother what he believes is her inert Holocaust consciousness: "'They're from Germany, you know,' I told her, squeezing her hand gently. 'Of course, I know,' Mom smiled, 'Adidas is the best brand in the world.' 'Grandpa was from Germany, too,' I tried to give her a hint. 'Grandpa was from Poland,' Mom corrected me."[27] The

---

24 Maya Jaggi, "Life at a Louder Volume," *The Guardian*, March 17, 2007, accessed August 8, 2018, https://www.theguardian.com/books/2007/mar/17/featuresreviews.guardianreview11.
25 Keret, "Shoes," 57.
26 Ibid.
27 Keret, "Shoes," 58.

brief conversation with the mother can be read as the second generation's repudiation of any attempt to impose Holocaust memory on their lives. Perhaps she chooses not to dwell on the painful past, namely, the murder of her father, so as not to upset her young son.

Yet, ultimately, it is apparent that she prefers to block and suppress that flow of memories that may disrupt the convenient patina of silence that she has adopted about this uncomfortable subject. Reminded of her father, she becomes sad for a moment, but that fleeting melancholy swiftly disappears. For her son, there is no ambiguity as to his mother's lack of empathy or understanding about the need for Holocaust commemoration, as we hear his thoughts about this key sequence: "I realised there was nothing doing. Mom didn't have a clue. She had never been to Volhynia House. Nobody had ever explained it to her. For her, shoes were just shoes and Germany was Poland. I let her put the shoes on me and didn't say a thing. There was no point in telling her and making her even sadder."[28]

The kinship with the survivor, and by extension with the grandfather, is amplified when the boy first looks at the shoebox. To him, the box resembles a coffin, and he anthropomorphizes the white shoes with the three blue stripes by likening them to dead Jews lying in repose. Further, as he wears the shoes, he notices the "pale hide covering my feet"[29] and immediately recollects the words of the old man. Likewise, when he touches the shoes' blue stripes, he associates them with the exhibit of the thin, old man that he dared touch in the museum, and the stripes echo the tears that ran down his cheeks "…like the divider lines you see on a highway.…"[30]

As he touches the shoes, the boy imagines the shoes to be his dead grandfather, and is concerned about treading on them or kicking the soccer ball: "I tiptoed slowly towards the door, trying to put as little weight as I could on the shoes…At the beginning of the game I still remembered not to kick with the tip of my shoe, so that it wouldn't hurt grandpa."[31] His reluctance to wear the shoes dissipates as he plays with his friends in the park. As he scores a goal, he not only feels comfortable, but believes that his grandfather is pleased with his performance on the field. Indeed, his initial principled opposition has given way to pride since the sneakers have oddly become connected to the unknown grandfather and have been reconstructed to exemplify intimacy: "'Some goal, eh?' I reminded grandpa on the way home. 'The goalie didn't know what hit him.' Grandpa said nothing,

---

28   Ibid.
29   Ibid.
30   Ibid., 56.
31   Ibid., 59.

but judging by the tread I could tell that he, too, was pleased."[32] The shoes become a means for the boy to bond with the absent grandfather, and fulfil a buried desire to recover an erased biographical family detail that has deliberately been expunged or hidden by the mother.

In the course of this offbeat and caustic tale, Keret presents an unusual moral twist that very few authors are likely to give us, avoiding the clichés of contemporary Israeli discourse. He convincingly limns the multiplex and labyrinthine emotional terrain evoked by Holocaust Memorial Day in young Israelis. The narrator oscillates between feelings of confusion, guilt, and—finally—pride, reminding us that there are no right responses to Holocaust memorialization and identification. It is in that spirit that Yael Feldman contends that the authors of the second generation reject:

> …the collective model of representation that they inherited from their parents and cultural mentors. Rather than finding 'the necessary link' that this model aspires to, contemporary writers seek a subjective encounter with the experiences that the ideology of this model suppressed. That they thereby undermine the historical closure assumed by that model is only too obvious.[33]

In a way, the young boy and his peers (who represent the third generation) are asked to walk in the shoes of those whose lives ended prematurely and tragically. Keret employs the motif of the shoes as a bold and subversive device to tackle the contentious and, for many, sacred issue of Holocaust monumentalization. Repeatedly, the shoes prompt the central protagonist to relive and recall the admonition ventured by the survivor in the Museum of Volhynia Jewry, namely, that German goods are made from the flesh of dead Jews. The considerable question as to whether to wear the shoes or not, or more specifically, whether to step on them, becomes the novel dilemma that the boy has to confront and ultimately resolve.

The boy believes the story told to him by the survivor that the shoes are made of his grandfather's dead body, and yet he rationalizes this imaginary fact as part of his own revenge on his peoples' brutalizers by assigning his newfound prowess on the sports field as a way of pleasing the murdered relative. By his own admission, the boy is guilty of the sin of forgetting what the old man counselled against when he begins to kick the ball with the

---

32   Ibid.
33   Yael S. Feldman, "Whose Story Is It, Anyway? Ideology and Psychology in the Representation of the Shoah in Israeli Literature," in *Probing the Limits of Representation: Nazism and the "Final Solution,"* ed. Saul Friedlander (Cambridge, MA: Harvard University Press, 1992), 238.

pointed end: "At the beginning of the game, I still remembered not to kick with the tip of the shoe, so that it wouldn't hurt grandpa, but after a while I forgot, just the old man at Volhynia House said people tend to do...."[34]

As the story concludes, the young boy has reconciled the competing pathways offered as appropriate forms of commemoration by preserving his bond with his grandfather, who he sincerely believes is part of the shoes manufactured in Germany. If the task is to never forget—as the old man maintains in his address ("People have short memories he said, but you won't forget. Every time you see a German, you'll remember what I told you"[35])—then the adolescent, in his whimsical and brash way, has fulfilled that vow. For Katzman, the evolution in the boy's sensibility and the intimacy he develops with the grandfather is nothing short of a modern miracle, especially since the hero overcomes and transcends the typical fettering and repressive signifiers of the Museum where his awareness in this subject is triggered.

In "Shoes," there is a glaring contrast between what is spoken about by the grown-ups, including teachers and eyewitnesses, concerning the terrible murders committed by the Nazis during the Holocaust and how it is understood by the young adults. On the one hand, when an elderly survivor rages against the Nazis and warns the schoolchildren in the hall not to visit Germany or purchase any German products, the boy only remembers the most superficial points that make no sense to him. He accepts the old man's claims that he once strangled a Nazi in revenge, convinced by the anger in his eyes. His classmate Djerby claims the old man is lying, unable to imagine the witness ever having been young and so charged with fury that this action is plausible. Djerby's remarks encapsulate the crippling attitudes held by many native Israelis in the first decades of statehood, in which the European Jews were seen as passive weaklings who were led to their death like "sheep to the slaughter" and never offered resistance to their Nazi persecutors.

That the young narrator should go on a school trip to the Museum of Volhynia for lessons on the Holocaust signals a dimension of Jewish history that extends beyond his immediate situation and age of awareness. This region in north-western Poland, skirting and sometimes overlapping with Ukraine, was the site for many significant events in Jewish history, such as the origins of the Hasidic movement, and the home of many important Jewish leaders, spiritual and lay. As well, this region resonates with Jews on a different level later in secular Jewish history as the site of

---

34   Keret, "Shoes," 59.
35   Ibid., 56.

pogroms, blood-libels, and other massacres. It is, in other words, a region soaked in bloodshed but also imbued with emotional ties for Polish and other Ashkenazi Jews. If the child narrator is tone deaf to all these resonances, intelligent adult readers cannot help but respond to the name of the Memorial Hall with powerful feelings.

Yet, at the same time, "Shoes" underlines the potential impact of survivor testimonies on young Israelis. It is of note that for years, the communal story of the Holocaust was that of the faceless mass of six million Jews, not of individuals who each had their own harrowing tale to narrate. The Shoah was compressed into the abstract number of six million, a generalizing model shorn of distinct and individual narratives that continuously erased the fragmentary nature of the atrocities. Although the initial delineation of the museum cues us to view it as alienating and cold—"Volhynia House was very beautiful and posh, all made of black marble, like millionaires' houses"[36]—it is obvious that the black-and-white pictures of the survivors and the impassioned speech by the old man prove more than just a cursory experience for the young man who refuses to participate in the collective process of suppression represented by his mother and father, who are willfully oblivious or select the modality of silence. A contrary reading is offered by Naveh, who argues that the story, undergirded by satire and parody,

> ...mocks the 'educational syllabus', the way it fulfils its aims, and reduces, cheapens and scorns the term 'second-generation' or 'the next generation' after the Holocaust'. The accomplishment of the boy in connecting with his grandfather is partly absurd since it is born out of series of mistakes. The visualization of the grandfather and his speech through the stupid conversation...are not, it would seem, a profound, conscious achievement.[37]

On the surface of the story, the name of the sport shoes that the boy has longed for and which soon become a point of moral dilemma insofar as he is old enough to understand the comments made by one of the survivor speakers at the Holocaust Memorial Day assembly merely indicates a product from Germany that should serve as a reminder of the atrocities committed against the Jews. Taking literally, but not too deeply, the warning that anything manufactured in Germany is likely to be made of the blood

---

36 Ibid., 55.
37 Hannah Naveh, *Nos'im ve-Nos'ot: Sipurey Mas'a ba-Sifrut ha-'Ivrit ha-Chadasha* [*Men and Women Travellers: Travel Narratives in Modern Hebrew Literature*] (Jerusalem: Misrad Habitachon, 2002), 262 (translation mine).

and bones of victims of the Shoah causes the boy to imagine that the pair of Adidas running shoes his parents have brought back from their trip to Europe is actually a remnant of his dead grandfather. The statement made in rage by the speaker at the memorial assembly that anyone who purchases or uses something made by the Germans is thereby acceding to the Nazi plan to exterminate all the Jews and turn their bodies into mere things was meant to be *hyperbole*—based on an extended figure of speech that collapses the distinction between a literal statement and a metaphorical one. Yet, it is also a form of synecdoche that takes a part for the whole—in this case, the generic name for a kind of apparel, for any and all things made by a German company. That declaration is understood in the boy's mind in such a way that the new shoes he puts on are a *fetish,* a symbolic object embodying the essence of his own ancestor, something that aids him in his prowess on the playing field and connects him with the consciousness and ghostly reappearance of his grandfather's body.

Several other factors are at play in regard to the Adidas shoes, though more problematically and obliquely. There is a historical ambiguity about the role the Adidas brothers and their factory played during the era of Nazi rule in Germany. Factors include how far they collaborated with the regime, their use of slave labor of Jews brought to concentration camps, and whether they were later were reeducated and rehabilitated. This is a personal and—as the boy's imaginary relations with the fetishized Adidas shoes further indicate—an emotional nexus, which is different from the historical lessons conveyed and the sense of moral outrage supposedly appropriate to the occasion of the Memorial Day events. A consequence of this suggested emotional bond between the grandfather and the grandson, one already dead and other growing to awareness of who and what he is as a Jew, is that the boy intuitively grasps that he is a child of Holocaust survivors, an heir to the promise of the State of Israel as a homeland and protective entity of Jews in the Diaspora: a promise that now that there is an Israel, there will never again be a Shoah since the Jewish state offers a shield to all Jews no matter where they are in the world and therefore something that he feels strongly enough to question his own parents' awareness of what all this means.

By bringing home the shoes that their son coveted, the parents have themselves transgressed the obligation to avoid anything made in Germany and, furthermore, for not realizing that the shoes are profoundly and intimately related to the grandfather who is perceived only as a cardboard photograph. However, the purchase of the shoes means that the grandfather can now be experienced as a living presence, one that imbues the grandchild with power on the sporting field and offers him some kind of supernatural protection, allowing him to break school rules.

Unlike his parents and older brother, and unlike the schoolteachers and other adults who try to bring to his attention the importance of Holocaust Memorial and of keeping the commandment of remembering, the survivor at the Museum of Volhynia speaks with an emotional intensity that the boy can understand, or thinks he can understand, as personal and visceral. The real man speaking in the hall, with all the passion of his experience, albeit mistaking the maturity of audience, is therefore more of a cardboard character in the story than the narrator's grandfather, whose presence he feels as a gut instinct within himself, as a living force in the life of his family, and then comically as an animated spirit in the Adidas shoes he wears.

Most important, "Shoes" represent an attempt to undermine and deconstruct predominant Israeli assumptions about post-Shoah identity. Hence, the work questions the adequacy of the official and sacrosanct frameworks produced by the state to portray the Holocaust as well as presenting alternate ways to delineating the legacy of the Holocaust. In more ways than one, Keret betrays a gritty spirit of rebellion against the statist appropriation of the Shoah and a vigorous desire to denationalize the Holocaust narrative and reclaim its personal and intimate dimension. In other words, what is at play here is an effort to privatize the traumatic memories of individuals that were collectivized by the state.

Bibliography

Aderet, Ofer. "Professor Gideon Greif Nilcham 'al Kvodo ha-'Avud shel Ka-Tzetnik." *Haaretz*, April 8, 2013.

Adorno, T.W. *Negative Dialectics*, translated by E. B Ashton. London: Continuum, 1981.

Alexander, Edward. *The Holocaust: History and the War of Ideas*. New Brunswick, NJ: Transaction Publishers: 1994.

---. *The Resonance of Dust: Essays on Holocaust Literature and Jewish Fate*. Columbus: Ohio State University Press, 1979.

Alexis, André. "Israel meets America: the mythic and the modern," *The Globe and Mail* (Canada), June 15, 2002: D29.

Alter, Robert. *Defenses of the Imagination: Jewish Writers and Modern Historical Crisis*. Philadelphia: Jewish Publication Society of America, 1976.

Appelfeld, Aharon. *Badenheim 1939*. London: J. M. Dent & Sons, 1980.

---. *Beyond Despair: Three Lectures and a Conversation with Philip Roth*. New York: Fromm International, 1994.

---. *Shanim ve-Sha'ot*. Tel Aviv: Hakibutz Hameuchad, 1975.

---. "The Awakening." In *Holocaust Remembrance: The Shapes of Memory*, edited by Geoffrey H. Hartman. Cambridge: Blackwell, 1994.

Arendt, Hannah. *Eichmann in Jerusalem: A Report on the Banality of Evil*. New York: Viking, 1963.

Balat, Avram. "Sipurei Yaldut 'Avuda," *Hatzofe*, July 2, 1978.

Band, Arnold J. "Foreword." In *Aharon Appelfeld: From Individual Lament to Tribal Eternity*, edited by Yigal Schwartz. Hanover and London: Brandeis University Press, 2001.

Bartov, Omer. *Mirrors of Destruction: War, Genocide, and Modern Identity*. New York: Oxford University Press, 2000.

Barzel, Hillel. *Ha-Me'ah ha-Ḥatsuyah: Mi-Modernizem le-Posṭ-Modernizem: Kerech 2: Monism ve-Pluralism*. Bnei Brak: Hakibutz Hameuchad and Sifriyat Hapoalim, 2013.

Bergman, Martin S., and Milton E. Jucovy, eds. *Generations of the Holocaust*. New York: Basic Books, 1982.

Bernstéin, Michael Andre. *Foregone Conclusions: Against Apocalyptic History*. Berkeley, CA: University of California Press, 1994.

Bonfil, Aliza-Corb. *Where Words are Silence*. Tel Aviv: Hakibutz Hameuchad, 2011.

Boyd, Tonkin. "How Aharon Appelfeld Chronicled the Holocaust," *The Independent*, May 19, 2012. Accessed August 8, 2018. https://www.independent.co.uk/arts-entertainment/books/features/how-aharon-appelfeld-chronicled-the-holocaust-7763595.html.

Brierly, William D. "Memory in the Work of Yehiel Dinur." In *Hebrew Literature in the Wake of the Holocaust*, edited by Leon Y. Yudkin. Rutherford, NJ: Fairleigh Dickinson University Press, 1993

Bryant, Thelma. "*Badenheim 1939* by Appelfeld." *The San Francisco Jung Institute Library Journal* 2, no. 3 (1981): 39-41.

Buddick, Emily Miller. *Aharon Appelfeld's Fiction: Acknowledging the Holocaust*. Bloomington: Indiana University Press, 2005.

Chertok. Haim. *We are All Close: Conversations with Israeli Writers*. New York: Fordham University Press, 1989

DeKoven Ezrahi, Sidra. *Booking Passage: Exile and Homecoming in the Modern Jewish Imagination*. Berkeley, CA: University of California Press, 2000.

Dror, Tzvika. "Ve-ha-Siyut Sholet Bo: Mifalo ha-Sifruti-Te'udi shel Ka-Tzetnik," *Davar*, April 20, 1990.

Drukker, Tamar S. "Language and Silences in two of Aharon Appelfeld's Coming-of-Age Tales." *Yod* 19 (2014): 1-10.

Engelhardt, Michael. "Adam Resurrected," *The Guardian*, December 13, 2008, accessed December 17, 2017, https://www.theguardian.com/books/2008/dec/14/fiction4

Eshel, Amir. "Eternal Present: Poetic Figuration and Cultural Memory in the Poetry of Yehuda Amichai, Dan Pagis and Tuvia Rubner." *Jewish Social Studies*, 7, no. 1 (2000): 141-166.

Feinberg, Anat. "Yoram Kaniuk." In *Encyclopedia Judaica*, vol. 11, 2nd ed., edited by Fred Skolnik. New York: Thomson Gale, 2007.

Feldman, Yael S. "Whose Story Is It, Anyway? Ideology and Psychology in the Representation of the Shoah in Israeli Literature." In *Probing the Limits of Representation: Nazism and the "Final Solution,"* edited by Saul Friedlander. Cambridge, MA: Harvard University Press, 1992.

Finkielkraut, Alain. *The Imaginary Jew*. London: University of Nebraska Press, 1994.

Friedlander, Saul, ed. "Trauma, Memory and Transference." In *Probing the Limits of Representation: Nazism and the "Final Solution,"* edited by Saul Friedlander. Cambridge, MA: Harvard University Press, 1992.

Fuchs, Esther. *Encounters with Israeli Authors*. Marblehead, MA: Micha Publications, 1982.

---. "Native Israeli Literature and the Spectre of Jewish History" (Fuchs Interview with Yoram Kaniuk). *Hebrew Book Review* 8, no. 1-2 (Fall/Winter, 1982–83): 60–61.

Giraldi, William. "Grasping for Words, Grappling with the Past," *The New Republic*, May 13, 2014. Accessed August 8, 2018. https://newrepublic.com/article/117739/aharon-appelfelds-suddenly-love-writing-and-holocaust.

Gluzman, Michael. "Memory without a Subject: About Dan Pagis and the Poetry of the State Generation." Paper delivered at symposium in memory of Professor Yosef Haefrati, June 17, 2007.

Goldberg, Amos, and Amos T. "An Interview with the Author Prof. Aharon Appelfeld," *Shoah Resource Center*, January 25, 1988.

Goldhagen, Daniel Jonah. *Hitler's Willing Executioners: Ordinary Germans and the Holocaust*. New York: Knopf, 1996.

Govrin, Nurit. "Mavo'." In *Kova' Zechuchit*, edited by Nava Semel. Tel Aviv: Sifriyat Hapoalim, 1985.

Grant, Linda. "Etgar Keret: Life: Try it Some Time," *The Independent*, February 25, 2005.

---. "Saturday Review: Essay: In the Zone of the Living," *The Guardian*, January 31, 2004

Green, David B. "Questions & Answers: A Conversation with Aharon Appelfeld," *Haaretz*, April 5, 2005. Accessed August 8, 2018. https://www.haaretz.com/life/books/1.5100334.

Green, Yaacov Jeffrey. "Appelfeld's Literary Art from the Point of View of the Translator." In *Between Frost and Smoke*, edited by Yitzhak Ben-Mordechai and Iris Parush. Be'er Sheva: Ben-Gurion University Press, 1997.

Greenberg, Uri Tzvi. "'Elohim! Hitzaltani me-'Ur-'Ashkenaz." In *Modern Hebrew Poetry: A Bilingual Anthology*, edited by Ruth Finer. Berkeley: University of California Press, 1996.

---. "Keter Kinah le-Kol Beit Israel." In *Rehovot ha-Nehar: Luach be-Mavo' 'Alef 'ad Shir me-lo ha-Yareach*, vol. 5, 46-59. Jerusalem: Bialik Institute, 1992.

---. "Le-'Elohim B-'Eiropa." In *Rehovot ha-Nehar: Luach be-Mavo' 'Alef 'ad Shir me-lo ha-Yareach*, vol. 6. Jerusalem: Bialik Institute, 1992.

---. "Lo Nidmenu le-Klavim bein ha-Goyim." In *Modern Hebrew Poetry: A Bilingual Anthology*, edited by Ruth Finer. Berkeley, CA: University of California Press, 1996.

---. *Rehovot ha-Nehar: Luach be-Mavo' 'Alef 'ad Shir me-lo ha-Yareach*. Jerusalem and Tel Aviv: Schoken, 1951.

---. "Shir ha-Ma'lach ha-Gadol," in *Rehovot ha-Nehar: Luach be-Mavo' 'Alef 'ad Shir me-lo ha-Yareach*, vol. 6. Jerusalem: Bialik Institute, 1992.

---. "Tachat Shen Macharashtam." In *Rehovot ha-Nehar: Luach be-Mavo' 'Alef 'ad Shir me-lo ha-Yareach*, vol. 6. Jerusalem: Bialik Institute, 1992.

Gubar, Susan. "The Long and the Short of Holocaust Verse." *New Literary History* 35, no. 3 (Summer 2004): 443-468.

Hagorni-Green, Avraham. *Be-Chavlei Shalom: Masot 'al ha-Shalom ve-ha-Shalem*. Jerusalem: Reches, 1994.

Hartman, Geoffrey. *The Longest Shadow: In the Aftermath of the Holocaust*. Bloomington, IN: Indiana University Press, 1996.

Harvey, Zev Warren. "Israeli Responses During and Following the War." In *Wrestling with God: Jewish Theological Responses During and After the Holocaust*, edited by Steven T. Katz, Shlomo Biderman, and Gershon Greenberg. Oxford: Oxford University Press, 2007.

Hatley, James. "Impossible Mourning: Two Attempts to Remember Annihilation." *The Centennial Review* 35, no. 3 (1991): 445-459.

Heftman, Yosef. "Beit ha-Bubot," *Haboker*, April 19, 1953.

Hirsch, David. "Review of *Foregone Conclusions: Against Apocalyptic History*." *Criticism* 37, no. 2 (Spring 1995): 335.

Hirsch, David. *The Destruction of Literature: Criticism after Auschwitz*. Hanover, NH: University Press of New England, 1991.

Hirsch, Marianne, and Leo Spitzer. "The War in the Archive: Holocaust Studies/Memory Studies." *Memory Studies* 2, no. 2 (May 2009): 151-170.

Holtzman, Avner. *Ahavot Tzion: Panim ba-Sifrut ha-'Ivrit ha-Chadasha*. Jerusalem: Carmel Publishing, 2006.

---. "Trends in Israeli Holocaust Fiction in the 1980s." *Modern Hebrew Literature* 8-9 (1992): 23-28.

Jacobson, David C., *Does David Still Play Before You? Israeli Poetry and the Bible*. Detroit, MI: Wayne State University, 1997.

---. "'Kill your Ordinary Common Sense and Maybe You'll Begin to Understand': Aharon Appelfeld and the Holocaust." *AJS Review* 13, no. 1-2 (Spring-Autumn 1988): 129-152.

Jacobs, Gerald. "The Jewish Literary Quarterly Awards." *Jewish Quarterly* 45, no. 1 (1998): 67.

Jaggi, Maya. "Life at a Louder Volume," *The Guardian*, March 17, 2007. Accessed August 8, 2018. https://www.theguardian.com/books/2007/mar/17/featuresreviews.guardianreview11.

Josipovici, Gabriel. "Writing the Unwritable: A Debate on Holocaust Fiction." *Jewish Chronicle* 45, no. 2 (1998): 12.

Ka-Tzetnik. *Haimut*. Tel Aviv: Hakibutz Hameuchad, 1987.
---. *Ha-Shaon asher me'al ha-Rosh*. Jerusalem: Mosad Bialik, 1960.
---. *Hatzofen*. Tel Aviv: Hakibutz Hameuchad, 1987.
---. *Salamandra*. Tel Aviv: Dvir, 1946.
---. *Shaon asher me'al ha-Rosh*. Tel Aviv: Hakibutz Hameuchad, 1989.
---. *Shivitti: A Vision*. Translated by Eliyah Nike de Nur and Lisa Herman. San Francisco: Harper and Row, 1987.
---. *Sunrise Over Hell*. London: W. H. Allen,1977.

Kaniuk, Yoram, *Adam Resurrected*. London: Atlantic Books, 2008.
---. *Ha-Yehudi ha-'Acharon*. Tel Aviv: Hakibutz Hameuchad and Sifriyat Hapoalim, 1982

Katz, Steven T., Shlomo Biderman, Gershon Greenberg, eds. *Wrestling with God: Jewish Theological Responses During and After the Holocaust*. Oxford: Oxford University Press, 2007.

Katzman, Roman. "Ga'aguim le-Mitos: 'Ishiyut, 'Etica, ve-'Ideologia ba-Mitopoesis shel Etgar Keret." *Mikan* 4 (January 2005): 20-41.

Keret, Etgar. *The Bus Driver Who Wanted to be God and Other Stories*. New York: Thomas Dunne, 2001.

---. "Shoes." *The Bus Driver Who Wanted to be God and Other Stories*. New York: Thomas Dunne, 2001.

Kliger, Noah. "Ha-Ish Mi-Kochav ha-'Efer Aushvitz," *Yediot Ahronot*, July 23, 2001.

Kraus, Nicole. "Born Again," *The New Yorker*, June 12, 2013. Accessed August 8, 2018. https://www.newyorker.com/books/page-turner/born-again.

Krull, Ryan, "The Rumpus Interview with Etgar Keret," *Rumpus*, July 27, 2015. Accessed August 8, 2018. http://therumpus.net/2015/07/the-rumpus-interview-with-etgar-keret/.

Kurzweil, Baruch. "Shirey Rechovot ha-Nehar." In *Rechovot ha-Nehar le Uri Zvi Greenberg: Mechkarim ve-Te'udot*, edited by Avidav Lipsker and Tamar Wolf-Monzon. Ramat Gan: Bar Ilan University Press, 2007.

LaCapra, Dominic. *Representing the Holocaust*. Ithaca: Cornell University Press, 1994.

Lang, Berel. *Act and Idea in the Nazi Genocide*. Chicago: The University of Chicago Press, 1990.

Lalor, Peter. "Twisted Reality Check," *The Daily Telegraph*, April 5, 2003.

Langer, Lawrence, ed. *Art from the Ashes: A Holocaust Anthology*. New York: Oxford University Press, 1995.

---. *Preempting the Holocaust*. New Haven, CT: Harvard University Press, 1998,

---. *The Holocaust and the Literary Imagination*. New Haven, CT: Yale University Press, 1975.

Lauper, Ruth. "*Ha-Dmama 'eina Horeshet Ra'*," *Haaretz*, February 23, 2003.

Lehmann-Haupt, Christopher. "Badenheim 1939," *New York Times*, December 9, 1980.

Lipsker, Avidov, and Avi Sagi, eds. *Twenty-Four Readings in Aharon Appelfeld's Literary Work*. Ramat Gan: Bar Ilan University Press and Shalom Hartman Institute, 2011.

---. 'Esrim ve-'Arba Rei'ot be-Kitvey Aharon A*ppelfeld*. Ramat Gan: Bar Ilan University Press, 2010.

Lyotard, Jean François. *The Differend: Phrases in Dispute*. Manchester: Manchester University Press, 1988.

Man Booker Prize, "Aharon Appelfeld," accessed August 18, 2016, http://themanbookerprize.com/author/aharon-appelfeld.

Mann, Itamar. "What is a 'Manifestly Illegal' Order? Law and Politics after Yoram Kaniuk's *Nevelot*." In *The Politics of Nihilism*, edited by Nitzan Lebovic and Roy Ben-Shai. London: Bloomsbury, 2014.

March, Michael. "A Saga of Jewish Sadness: A Conversation with Aharon Appelfeld." *The New Presence* (September 1997): 16-17.

Megged, Aharon. "I Was Not There." In *Comprehending the Holocaust: Historical and Literary Research*, edited by Asher Cohen, Yoav Gelber, and Charlotte Wardi. New York: Peter Lang, 1988.

Milner, Iris. *Kirchey 'Avar: Biografiya, Zehut ve-Zicharon be-Siporet ha-Dor ha-Sheni*. Tel Aviv: Am Oved, 2003.

---. "The 'Gray Zone' Revisited: The Concentrationary Universe in Ka. Tzetnik's Literary Testimony," *Jewish Social Studies* 14, no. 2 (Winter 2008): 113-155.

Mintz, Alan, ed. *Reading Hebrew Literature: Critical Discussions of Six Modern Texts*. Hanover: Brandeis University Press, 2003.

Miron, Dan. *Hasifriya ha-'Ivrit: Proza Me'urevet: 1980-2005*. Tel Aviv: Miskal/Yediot Ahronoth Books and Chemed Books, 2005.

Mirsky, David. "The Noose Slowly Tightens," *Southern Jewish Weekly*, September 25, 1981.

Mitgang, Herbert. *Words Still Count With Me: A Chronicle of Literary Conversations*. New York: W. W. Norton & Co, 1995.

---. "Writing Holocaust Memories," *The New York Times*, November 15, 1986.

Morahg, Gilead. "Breaking Silence: Israel's Fantastic Fiction of the Holocaust." In *The Boom in Contemporary Israeli Fiction*, edited by Alan Mintz. Hanover: University Press of New England, 1997.

Naparstek, Ben. "Interview with Etgar Keret." *Tikkun* 20, no. 5 (September/October 2005): 70-71.

Nash, Stanley. "A Creative Sense of Impasse: Aharon Appelfeld's *Essays in the First Person*." *Modern Hebrew Literature*, 7, no. 1-2 (Winter 1981-1982): 56-59.

Naveh, Hannah. *Nos'im ve-Nos'ot: Sipurey Mas'a ba-Sifrut ha-'Ivrit ha-Chadasha*. Jerusalem: Misrad Habitachon, 2002.

Needler, Howard. "Red Fire Upon Black Fire: Hebrew in the Holocaust Novels of K. Tsetnik." In *Writing in the Holocaust*, edited by Berel Lang. New York: Holmes and Meier, 1988.

Nizkor Project. "The Trial of Adolf Eichmann, Session 68." Accessed December 24, 2017. http://www.nizkor.org/hweb/people/e/eichmann-adolf/transcripts/Sessions/Session-068-01.html.

O'Keeffe, Alice. "Etgar Keret: Israelis Boycott me as a Traitor, and Foreigners because I'm Israeli." *The Guardian*, August 1, 2015. Accessed August 8 2018. https://www.theguardian.com/books/2015/aug/01/etgar-keret-books-interview-israel-the-seven-good-years.

Ovadyahu, Mordechai. "Mesaper ha-Planeta ha-Shchora: Ka-Tzetnik (Yehiel Dinur)." In *Be-Sa'ar u-vi-Dmama: Demuyut be-Sifrutenu ha-Chadasha*, edited by Mordechai Ovadyahu. Tel Aviv: Alef, 1976.

Parson, Ann. "Interview: Aharon Appelfeld." *Boston Review* (December 1982). Accessed August 8, 2018. http://bostonreview.net/archives/BR07.6/appelfeld.html.

Plank, Karl. *Mother of the Wire Fence: Inside and Outside the Holocaust*. Louisville, KY: Westminster John Knox Press, 1994.

Popkin, D. Jeremy. "Katzetnik 135633: The Survivor as Pseudonym." *New Literary History* 33, no. 2 (Spring 2002): 343-355.

"PM Netanyahu's Speech at Plenary Meeting Marking 50 Years Since the Eichmann Trial," *Prime Minister's Office*, December 13, 2011.

Ramras-Rauch, Gila. *Aharon Appelfeld: The Holocaust and Beyond*. Indianapolis: Indiana University Press, 1994.

---. "Dan Pagis." In *Encyclopedia of Holocaust Literature*, edited by David Patterson, Alan L. Berger, and Sarita Cargas. Westport, CT: Oryx Press, 2002.

Rosen, Norma. *Accidents of Influence*. Albany: State University of New York Press, 1992: 47.

Roskies, David G. *Against the Apocalypse: Responses to Catastrophe in Modern Jewish Culture*. Cambridge, MA: Harvard University Press, 1984.

---, ed. *The Literature of Destruction: Jewish Responses to Catastrophe*. Philadelphia: Jewish Publication Society, 1988.

Roskies, David G., and Naomi Diamant. *Holocaust Literature: A History and Guide*. Waltham, MA: Brandeis University Press, 2012.

Roth, John K. "On Seeing the Invisible Dimensions of the Holocaust." *Holocaust and Genocide Studies* 1, no. 1 (1986): 147-153.

Rovner, Adam. "Instituting the Holocaust: Comic Fiction and the Moral Career of the Survivor." *Jewish Culture and History* 5, no. 2 (2000): 11.

Rudolf, Anthony. "Obituary: Ka-Tzetnik 135633," *The Independent*, July 27, 2001.

Schneider, Schmuel. *Existence and Memory: In the Writings of Aharon Appelfeld and Yosef Chaim Brenner and Other Writings*. Jerusalem: Carmel, 2010.

Schwartz, Daniel R. "Aharon Appelfeld's Parables." In *Imagining the Holocaust*, edited by Daniel R. Schwartz. New York: St. Martin's Press, 1999.

Schwartz, Yigal, and Jeffrey M. Green. "Person, the Path, and the Melody: A Brief History of Identity in Israeli Literature." *Prooftexts* 20, no. 3 (Fall 2000): 327.

Schwartz, Yigal. *Kinat ha-Yachid ve-Netzach ha-Shevet: Aharon Appelfeld—Tmunat 'Olam*. Jerusalem: Keter, 1996.

Segev, Tom. "Met ha-Sofer Yehiel Dinur, aval K.Tzetnik Yichye la-Netzach," *Haaretz*, July 18, 2001.

---. "The code of Ka. Tzetnik," *Koteret Rashit*, May 27, 1987.

---. *The Seventh Million: The Israelis and The Holocaust*. New York: Hill and Wang, 1993.

Shabbat-Nadir, Hadas, and Yigal Schwartz. "Dan Pagis." In *Lexicon Heksherim le-Sofrim Yisraelim*, edited by Stavi Zisi and Yigal Schwarz. Beer Sheva: Kinneret, Zmora Bitan, Dvir Publishing House and Heksherim Institute for Jewish and Israeli Literature and Culture, 2014.

Shacham, Chaya. *Bedek Bayit: 'Al Levatey Zehut, Ideologia ve-Cheshbon Nefesh ba-Sifrut ha-'Ivrit ha-Chadasha*. Sde Boker: Machon ben Gurion, 2012.

Shaked, Gershon. *Gal Chadash ba-Siporet ha-'Ivrit: Mason 'al Siporet Yisraelit Tzeira*. Tel Aviv: Sifriyat Hapoalim, 1970.

---. *Modern Hebrew Literature*. New Milford: Toby Press, 2008.

Shapir, Alan. *That Self-Forgetful Perfectly Useless Concentration*. Chicago and London: The University of Chicago Press, 2016.

Shavit, Yaacov. "Eschatology and Politics: Between 'A Great Prophesy' and 'A Small Prophesy'—the Case of Uri Zvi Greenberg." In *Ha'matkonet Ve'Hadmut: Studies on the Poetry of Uri Zvi Greenberg*, edited by H. Weiss. Ramat Gan: Bar Ilan University, 2000.

---. "Uri Zvi Greenberg: Conservative Revolutionarism and National Messianism." *The Jerusalem Quarterly* 48 (Fall 1988): 63-72.

Shnitzer, Shmuel. "The Eichmann Trial in Jerusalem," *Maariv*, June 8, 1961.

Shoffman, Gershon. *The Complete Writings of G. Shoffman*, vol. 4. Tel Aviv: Am Oved, 1962.

Silberschlag, Eisig. *From Renaissance to Renaissance II: Hebrew Literature in the Land of Israel 1870-1970*. New York: Ktav Publishing House, 1977.

Shindler, Colin. *The Rise of the Israeli Right: From Odessa to Hebron*. New York: Cambridge University Press, 2015.

Shorer, Haim. "To the Prosecutor in the Eichmann Trial: About a Terrible and Holy Book." *Davar*, June 1961, 21.

Sinclair, Clive. "ICA Guardian Conversation: Aharon Appelfeld with Clive Sinclair." Video. 1987. Accessed August 8, 2018. https://www.kanopystreaming.com/product/aharon-appelfeld-clive-sinclair.

Smith, Erin. "'Written in Pencil in the Sealed Boxcar': Voices from the Periphery." *Xenophile: A Journal of Comparative Literature* 2 (April 25, 2014): 16-18.

Sokoloff, Naomi, "Holocaust Transformations in Dan Pagis's *Gilgul*." *Hebrew Annual Review* 8 (1984): 215-240.

Spicehandler, Ezra. "Greenberg, Uri Zevi." In *Encyclopedia Judaica*, vol. 8, 2nd ed., edited by Fred Skolnik. New York: Thomson Gale, 2007.

Stahl, Netta. "'Man's Red Soup'—Blood and the Art of Esau in the Poetry of Uri Zvi Greenberg." In *Jewish Blood: Reality and Metaphor in History, Religion and Culture*, edited by Mitchell B. Hart. New York: Routledge, 2009.

Strassler, David. "The Heroes of Ammunition Hill," *The Jerusalem Post*, May 12, 1991.

Streitfeld, David. "Imagining the Unimaginable," *The Washington Post*, January 10, 1999.

Szeintuch, Yehiel. *K. Zetnik 135633: A Series of Dialogues with Yehiel Dinur*. Jerusalem: Beit Lochamei Hagetaot/Dov Sadan Institute, 2003.

---. "Discerning key terms in the Writings of K. Zetnik." *Hulyot: Studies in Yiddish Literature and its links with Hebrew literature* 5 (1999): 275-290.

Temkin, Moshe. "One Happy Camper," *The Jerusalem Post*, March 29, 1999.

"The Charles Bronfman Prize Names Etgar Keret as 2016 Recipient." Accessed August 8, 2018. https://thecharlesbronfmanprize.org/pressreleases/the-charles-bronfman-prize-names-etgar-keret-as-2016-recipient/.

Toker, Leona. "Truth and testimony," *Haaretz*, March 26, 2003.

Wardi, Dina. *Memorial Candles*. London and New York: Routledge, 1992.

White, Hayden. "Historical Emplotment and the Problem of Truth." In *Probing the Limits of Representation: Nazism and the "Final Solution,"* edited by Saul Friedlander. Cambridge, MA: Harvard University Press, 1992.

Weingrad, Michael. "An unknown Yiddish masterpiece that anticipated the Holocaust," *Mosaic*, April 15, 2015. Accessed August 8, 2018. https://mosaicmagazine.com/observation/2015/04/an-unknown-yiddish-masterpiece-that-anticipated-the-holocaust/.

Weiss Halivni, David. "Holocaust questions." *Judaism: A Quarterly Journal of Jewish Life and Thought* 46, no. 4 (Fall 1997): 474-477.

Whitman, Ruth. "Motor Car, Bomb, God: Israeli Poetry in Translation." *The Massachusetts Review* 23, no. 2 (Summer 1982): 309-328.

Wiesel, Elie. "Some Questions that Remain Open" in *Comprehending the Holocaust: Historical and Literary Research*, edited by Asher Cohen, Yoav Gelber, and Charlotte Wardi. New York: Peter Lang, 1988.

Wisse, Ruth. "Aharon Appelfeld, Survivor," *Commentary*, August 1, 1983, 74-76.

Wolf-Monzon, Tamar, and Zohar Livnat. "The Poetic Codes of Rechovot Ha-Nahar ('Streets of the River')." *Shofar* 23, vol. 2 (Winter 2005): 19-33.

Yablonka, Hanna. *The State of Israel vs. Adolf Eichmann*. New York: Schocken Books, 2004.

Yaoz, Hanna. "Holocaust Hebrew Literature—Between the Concrete and the Mythological" in *Comprehending the Holocaust: Historical and Literary Research*, edited by Asher Cohen, Yoav Gelber and Charlotte Wardi. New York: Peter Lang, 1998.

Yerushalmi, Haim Yosef. *Zakhor: Jewish History and Jewish Memory*. Seattle: University of Washington Press, 1998.

Young, James E. *Writing and Rewriting the Holocaust: Narrative and the Consequences of Interpretation*. Bloomington: Indiana University Press, 1988.

Yuter, Alan, J. *The Holocaust in Hebrew Literature: From Genocide to Rebirth*. New York and Port Washington: Associated Faculty Press, 1983.

Yudkin, Leon Y., ed. *Hebrew Literature in the Wake of the Holocaust*. Rutherford, NJ: Fairleigh Dickinson University Press, 1993.

---. *A Home Within: Varieties of Jewish Expressions in Modern Fiction*. Middlesex: Symposium Press, 1998.

---. "Narrative Perspectives in Holocaust Literature." In *Hebrew Literature in the Wake of the Holocaust*, edited by Leon Y. Yudkin. Rutherford, NJ: Fairleigh Dickinson University Press, 1993.

Zierler, Wendy. "Footprints, Traces, Remnants: The Operations of Memory in Dan Pagis's Aqebot." *Judaism* 41, no. 4 (Fall 1992): 316-333.

Index

Abel, 33-36, 39,
Adam, 34-36, 41
Adorno, Theodor, x, 58, 112
   Negative Dialectics, 58, 112
Al ha-Mishmar, 32
Alexis, André, xviii, 112
   Israel meets America: the mythic and the modern, xviii
Allied Nuremberg Trials, 26
Alighieri, Dante, 101
Alter, Robert, 42-43, 48, 112
   Defenses of the Imagination: Jewish Writers and Modern Historical Crisis, 43
Anschluss, 9, 19, 21, 25-27, 29
Appelfeld, Aharon, xiv, 1-9, 12-16, 18, 20-27, 29-30, 112-120
   Badenheim 1939, xiv, 7-9, 12-13, 15, 16, 18-26, 28-30, 112, 113, 116
   Beyond Despair: Three Lectures and a Conversation with Philip Roth, 13-14, 27, 112
   Shanim ve-Sha'ot, 7, 112
   The Awakening, 7, 112
Appelfeld, Michael, 4
Arendt, Hannah, 16, 26, 112,
   Eichmann in Jerusalem 16, 25, 26
Asherman, Nina, 78
Auschwitz, vii, x, xiii, xv, xvii, xix, 15, 21, 29, 33, 35, 46, 53, 67, 75-83, 85-87, 89-96, 103, 115
Auslander, Judith, 31
Austria, 9-10, 19, 21, 24, 26, 29-30

Bartov, Omer, 77, 112
   Mirrors of Destruction: War, Genocide, and Modern Identity, 77, 112
Barzel, Hillel, 11, 112
   Ha-Me'ah ha-Ḥatsuyah: Mi-Modernizem le-Posṭ-Modernizem: Kerech 2: Monism ve-Pluralism, 11, 112
Ben Gurion University of the Negev, 6
Bernstéin, Michael Andre, 22-25, 112
   Foregone Conclusions: Against Apocalyptic History 23, 25, 112, 115
Bilkamin, 42
Bonfil, Aliza-Corb, 47, 113
   Where Words are Silence, 47, 113
Bukovina, xiv, 4, 31,

Cain, 34-41, 68
Charles Bronfman Prize, 101-102, 119
Chernovtsy, 4, 6
Ravikovitch, Dahlia, 32

David, 66
Dinur, Daniella, 78, 87
Dinur, Lior 78
Dinur, Yehiel, Ka-Tzetnik 135633, xv, 75-76, 78-85, 87-94, 96, 112-113, 117-119
   Beit Habubot, House of Dolls, xv, 81, 87, 90
   Ha-Shaon asher me'al ha-Rosh, Star Eternal 15, 81, 93-94, 115
   Hatzofen, 115
   Salamandra, Sunrise over Hell, xv, 79, 81-83, 86, 90, 115
   Shivitti: A Vision, 78, 105, 115
   Qaru Lo Piepel, Atrocity, xv, 81, 90-91

Eichmann Trial, xv, 72, 75, 79-81, 90
Eshel, Amir, 38-39, 113,
Ezrahi, Dekoven, 40, 113
   Booking Passage: Exile and Homecoming in the Modern Jewish Imagination, 40, 113

Feinberg, Anat, 55, 113
   Yoram Kaniuk, 55, 113

German Reich, 9
Gluzman, Michael, 32, 113-114
   Memory without a Subject: About Dan Pagis and the Poetry of the State Generation, 32, 113-114
Goldberg, Leah, 32, 114
Goldberg, Amos, 21, 113
Goldhagen, Daniel, 41, 114
   Hitler's Willing Executioners: Ordinary Germans and the Holocaust, 41, 114
Green, B., David, 5, 114
   Questions & Answers: A Conversation with Aharon Appelfeld, 5, 114
Green, Jeffrey M., 20, 56, 118
   Person, the Path, and the Melody: A Brief History of Identity in Israeli Literature, 56, 118
Greenberg, Uri Zvi, xv-xvi, 3, 42, 43-53, 76, 119
   Elohim! Hitzaltani me-'Ur-'Ashkenaz, Lord! You Saved Me from Ur-Germany As I Fled, 53, 114
   Keter Kinah le-Kol Beit Israel, A Crown of Lament for All of the House of Israel, 47
   Le-'Elohim B-'Eiropa, 114
   Lo Nidmenu le-Klavim bein ha-Goyim, 114
   Rehovot ha-Nehar: Luach be-Mavo, Streets of the River, 47, 114
   Shir ha-Ma'lach ha-Gadol, The Song of the Great March, 50, 51, 114
   Tachat Shen Macharashtam, Under the Tooth of their Plough, 48, 51, 114
Greif, Gideon, 76, 112

Hartmann, Geoffrey, xii
Harvey, Warren Zev, 76, 115
   Israeli Responses During and Following the War, 76, 115
Hatley, James, 18, 28-29, 115
   Impossible Mourning: Two Attempts to Remember Annihilation, 18, 115
Hausner, Gideon, 79- 81, 90
Hebrew University of Jerusalem, 6, 32
Hirsh, David, 25-26
Holtzman, Avner, 3-4, 99, 115
   Ahavot Tzion: Panim ba-Sifrut ha-'Ivrit ha-Chadasha, 3, 115

International Red Cross, 12
Israel, vii, xvi-1, 3, 31, 39, 40, 41, 43-45, 47, 49, 52-58, 60-62, 64-66, 70-71, 73, 77, 80-81, 86, 90, 96-99, 101-103, 105, 107, 109-112, 114, 117, 119-120,
Italy, 6, 78, 82

Jacobs, Gerald, 98, 115
   The Jewish Literary Quarterly Awards, 98, 115
Jacobson, David C., 12, 33,
Jewish Brigade, 78

Kaniuk, Yoram, xvi-xvii, 54-57, 59-60, 66-67, 72, 113, 115
   Adam Resurrected, xvi, 54-59, 73, 113, 115
   Ha-Yehudi ha-'Acharon, The Last Jew, 55, 115
Katz, Reuben,
Keret, Etgar, xvii-xviii, 97, 101-105, 107-108, 111, 114, 116-119
   Shoes, xvii, 16, 976 103-104, 108, 110-111, 115
Kerouac, Jack, 99
Kliger, Noah, xv, 116
   Ha-'Ish mi-Kokav Ha-'Efer Aushvitz
Kraus, Nicole, 54, 116
Kristallnacht, 30
Kurzweil, Baruch, xvi, 116
   Shirey Rechovot ha-Nehar, xvi, 116

Langer, Lawrence L., xix, 34-35, 100, 116
   Art from the Ashes: A Holocaust Anthology, 35, 116
   Preempting the Holocaust, xix, 100, 116
   The Holocaust and the Literary Imagination, 34, 116
Lehmann-Haupt, Christopher, 12, 116
Lipsker, Avidov, xvi, 1, 23-24, 43, 49, 53
Lublin, 77, 116

Mann, Thomas, 73
Merhavia, 32, 116
Miller Budick, Emily, 25
   Aharon Appelfeld's Fiction: Acknowledging the Holocaust, 25
Milner, Iris, xvii, 25, 55-56, 117
   Avar: Biografiya, Zehut ve-Zicharon be-Siporet ha-Dor ha-Sheni xvii, 117
   The 'Gray Zone' Revisited: The Concentrationary Universe in Ka. Tzetnik's Literary Testimony, 56, 117

Mintz, Alan, 3, 45, 117
  Reading Hebrew Literature: Critical Discussions of Six Modern Texts, 3, 45, 117
Miron, Dan, 3-4, 77, 82, 117
  Hasifriya ha-'Ivrit: Proza Me'urevet: 1980-2005, 3-4, 77, 82, 117
Mount Sinai, 53-54

Nash, Stanley, 12, 117
Needler, Howard, 91-92, 117
  Red Fire Upon Black Fire, 91-92, 117
Netanyahu, Benyamin, 80

Orlogin, 32

Pagis, Dan, xiv, 31-35, 39, 41, 113-114
Palestine, 5-6, 31,42, 53-54, 65, 78-79, 84, 86
Plank, Karl, 37, 118
  Mother of the Wire Fence: Inside and Outside the Holocaust, 37, 118
Poland, 10-11, 13-14, 15, 17, 20, 22, 24, 30, 42, 45, 49, 68, 77, 84, 87, 94, 101, 102, 105, 106, 108
Proust, Marcel, 5
  Remembrance of Things Past, 5

Radauiti, 31
Ramras Rauch, Gila, 2, 14, 21, 31
Romania, 4, 31
Roskies, David, x, 44, 48-49, 117
Roth, John K., 93, 118
  On Seeing the Invisible Dimensions of the Holocaust, 93, 118
Roth, Philip, 13, 26, 112
Rovner, Adam, 57, 118
  Instituting the Holocaust: Comic Fiction and the Moral Career of the Survivor, 57, 118
Ruebner, Tuvia, 32

Sagi, Avi,1, 23- 24
Schneider, Schmuel, 2, 3, 27, 101, 118
  Existence and Memory: In the Writings of Aharon Appelfeld and Yosef Chaim Brenner and Other Writings, 3, 27, 101, 118
Schwartz, Yigal, 8, 33, 56, 118
  Aharon Appelfeld: From Individual Lament to Tribal Eternity, 8, 33, 56, 118
Segev, Tom, 78, 79, 82, 90, 118
  The Author Yehiel Dinur is Dead, but Ka-Tzetnik will Live Forever, 78
  The Seventh Million, 82, 90, 118
  The code of Ka. Tzetnik, 79
Shavit, Uri, 45-46
Shoffman, Gershon, 83, 87, 119
  The Complete Writings of G. Shoffman, 83, 87, 119
Shorer, Haim, 90, 119
  To the Prosecutor in the Eichmann Trial: About a Terrible and Holy Book, 90, 119
Silberschlag, Eisig, 43, 119
Sinclair, Clive, 16, 119
Six-Day War, xvi
Smith, Eric, 34
  Written in Pencil in the Sealed Boxcar': Voices from the Periphery, 34
Sokoloff, Naomi, 38-39, 119
  Holocaust Transformations in Dan Pagis's Gilgul, 39, 119
Solzhenitsyn, Aleksandr, 73
  Cancer Ward, 73
Sosnowiec, 77
Spicehandler, Ezra, 43-44, 49, 119
SS, Schutzstaffel, 12, 85, 88
Stahl, Neta, 46, 119
  Man's Red Soup'—Blood and the Art of Esau in the Poetry of Uri Zvi Greenberg, 46, 119
Steiner, Adam, 73
Steiner, George, x
Sternberg, Bunia, 4
Switzerland, 58, 65, 83

Tel-Aviv, 70
Terra-Viso, 78
Theresienstadt Ghetto, 11
Toker, Leona, 77, 119
  Truth and Testimony, 77, 119
Transnistria, 6, 31
Treblinka, 15

Ukraine, 4, 108

Wannsee Conference, 71
War of Independence, 6, 54
Weiss Halivni, David, xi, 120
  Holocaust questions, xi, 120
White, Haydn, xiii, xiv, 120
  Historical Emplotment and the Problem of Truth, xiii, xiv, 120
Whitman, Ruth, 35, 120

Motor Car, Bomb, God: Israeli Poetry in Translation, 35, 120
Whitman, Walt, 46
Wiesel, Elie, xix, 120
Some Questions that Remain Open, xix, 120
Wisse, Ruth, 23, 120
Aharon Appelfeld, Survivor, 23

Yarkon River, 70
Amichai, Yehuda, 32, 39, 113
Yizrael Valley, 32
Yudkin, Leon, ix, 76, 113, 120
Hebrew Literature in the Wake of the Holocaust, ix, 76, 113, 120
Yuter, Arnold J., 39, 90, 120
The Holocaust in Hebrew Literature: From Genocide to Rebirth, 39, 90, 120

Zhadova, 4
Zierler, Wendy, 38, 120
Footprints, Traces, Remnants: The Operations of Memory in Dan Pagis's Aqebot, 38, 120

www.ingramcontent.com/pod-product-compliance
Lightning Source LLC
Chambersburg PA
CBHW050113170426
43198CB00014B/2556